Hello metal friends! This book is full of information and stories that just didn't quite fit in our feature book: **Soundtrack of our Youth**, which was ballooning up to almost 500 pages.

Demos and B-Sides is full of more fun information. The Hair Metal Hall of Fame is probably the coolest aspect. Plus exclusive interviews with the bands Hardcore Superstar and Love Razer, as well as with lead singer Chad Cherry of The Last Vegas and Shameless founder Alexx Michael.

We also focus a lot of the 2000s, as well as the more underrated bands, songs and album of the hair metal genre.

We hope you enjoy the information in this book!

Underrated
Bands
Songs
Billboard Chart History
Current Bands Kicking Ass
Dudes Who Deserve More Credit
Chad Cherry interview
Alexx Michael interview
Hardcore Superstar interview
Love Razer interview
Max Perenchio interview
Dito Godwin
Mutt and Desmond – Hit Makers
To Songs/albums 2000-2017
Fan pictures, tattoos and stories
Online music sites

UNDERRATED

We don't like to use the adjectives underrated or overrated when describing bands, albums or songs. Realistically, bands achieve the exact success they earned and deserved. When fans say a band is underrated what they really mean is that they just personally love that band more than everybody else does. Same thing with overrated. It just means a fan doesn't like a band that everybody else likes.

So we'll go with the description that these are bands that put out some great albums that didn't receive the same amount of popularity (and publicity) as some of their contemporaries. Maybe they got lost in the shuffle or came out a couple years too late. Possibly they didn't have the right look or they didn't receive major backing from their label.

These are bands that we feel should have achieved more success. Bands that were more talented than the success level they earned. In this book, this is the section where a bit of our personal bias comes through.

Also, we must specify that these are bands that any self respecting hair metal fan has heard of and probably owns at least a couple of their albums. Unlike the bands in the list below this one, we know this list features prominent bands from the era. These are just the guys we thought should have been bigger.

BANDS

1. D-A-D

Danish based D-A-D might be the best rock band that you've never heard of. Or maybe you have heard of them, but didn't dig into their catalog after listening to their biggest hit – Sleeping My Day Away. SMDA is a fun song with an infectious groove but sort of cheesy in the lyrics department.

But don't worry if that was you! Today is your lucky day. We are demanding that you take the next two hours and delve deep into D-A-D's catalog. There is a 94% chance you'll become a fan for life.

D-A-D has been in existence since 1982 and have released 11 studio albums. They are known for Jesper Binzer's raspy vocals and lyrics that are more "fun" than sexual or morose. Another fun fact, the band has more name changes than member changes in their 36-year history. Jesper and Jacob Binzer, Stig Pederson have been members since the beginning. Drummer Laust Sonne replaced Peter Jensen in 1999. That's it.

D-A-D has 15 songs listed in our Top 1,000 list. Key songs include Girl Nation, Between You and Me, Laugh 'N' a ½ and the aforementioned Sleeping My Day Away.

2. Junkyard
The band with the hardest sound to describe. Sleazy? Bluesy? Southern rock? Boogie-woogie country-rock? Punk? That's the real beauty of Junkyard. While fitting perfectly into the sleaze metal era, Junkyard brought a new, fresh and unique sound to the genre.

Junkyard's heart and soul is lead singer and primary songwriter David Roach. Roach is pure punk to the core. Junkyard's two more popular songs are the smooth, sweet sounding Hollywood and Simple Man. But don't expect to see a hair band if you attend a Junkyard show. A great example of what Roach and Junkyard are all about is how Roach handles a crowd. We attended a recent Junkyard show that was starting to be marred by two hardcore Junkyard fans, who also happened to be extremely drunk and obnoxious. They were bumping into people, barging their way to the front row and causing havoc in the crowd. Fans were calling for the bouncers to remove the hooligans.

So what happened? Roach went face-to-face with the most obnoxious one. Grabbed him by the hand and pulled the guy so they were just inches away. With sweat flying, spit spraying, Roach spent about 20 seconds just absorbing all of the fan's crazy energy into himself. Whereas an Axl Rose or Sebastian Bach would have had the fan tossed from the venue, Roach took it upon himself to keep the show positive and all about the fans. It was an amazing sight to see.

Their self-titled album is a classic. Released in 1989 it features four really fantastic songs. The aforementioned Simple Man, Hollywood as well as Blooze and Hands Off. Other standout tracks include the amazing ballad Slipping Sway from their 1991 album *Sixes, Sevens and Nines*.

Junkyard has thirteen songs in our top 1,000 list, as well as releasing five must own albums: *Junkyard, Joker, Tried and True, High Water and Sixes, Sevens and Nines*.

3. Dangerous Toys
Texas-based bands make up two of the top three spots on the list. Legendary singer Jason McMaster and Dangerous Toys were the genre's closest thing to Guns N' Roses. If you love Axl and GnR, Skid Row, Cinderella…as well as non-genre bands like AC/DC and Metallica – then Dangerous Toys should fill your iPod playlist.
How to officially describe Dangerous Toys? Simple. They kick your ass. End of story.

They have nine songs in the top 1,000, including an extremely respectful seven inside the top 200 (five on the rock side, two on the ballad side).

Scared and Teas'n Pleas'n were their most popular tunes. But every HM/HB fan needs to immediately check out Screamin' For More, Queen of the Nile and Angel N U.

Key albums include their self-titled debut, *Hellacious Acres* and *Pissed*.

Just an amazing band that should have ended up being way bigger.

4. Tora Tora
Describing a band's sound as being blues-based became a bit of a cliché towards the end of the height of the Sleaze Metal era. It was an easy way to try and distinguish the band from the glam, make-up look/sound that was falling out of favor with fans. One band that truly did embrace the blues-rock sound more so than their typical counterparts were the fantastic Tora Tora. They were the cream of the crop of blues-based rock.

And another brilliant thing about Tora Tora? Thirty years later they might be the only major HM/HB band out there that is still touring with their original members. For comparison, L.A. Guns has featured – no joke – more than 40 different line-ups. Major props to Anthony Corder, Keith Douglas, Patrick Francis and John Patterson for sticking together.

Tora Tora has 15 songs featured in our Top 1,000 songs, including standouts like Walkin' Shoes, Wild America, Phantom Rider and Being There. Key albums include *Surprise Attack, Wild America, Revolution Day* and *Miss B Haven*.

5. Babylon A.D.
Derek Davis has one of the most underrated voices in the genre. And unlike a lot of his peers, Davis still sounds great today. Babylon's debut album featured two of the best songs of the era – Bang Goes the Bell and Desperate (rated as a top 30 ballad on our list).

The band scored nine songs in our top 1,000 list. Key albums include their self-titled debut, *American Blitzkrieg* and *Fool on Fire*.

6. Vain
Either you love Davy Vain's voice…..or you don't. But if you are a fan, Vain has put out seven pretty quality albums since their 1989 debut *No Respect*. They charted 15 songs on our top 1,000 list.

7. Killer Dwarfs
Even a gnarly car wreck hasn't been able to stop vocalist Russ Graham from kicking ass on stage. Killer Dwarfs are one of the top rock bands to ever come out of Canada. They have released six albums and have six songs on our list.

8. Arcade
One of the first "super groups" from the genre. Ratt frontman Stephen Pearcy and Cinderella drummer Fred Coury put out two quality albums in the early 90s. Five songs made our Top 1,000 list, including the beautiful ballad Mother Blues.

9. Every Mother's Nightmare
They had one great song – Love Can Make You Blind – but mainly EMN just put out a bunch of solid rock n' roll albums. They have five songs on our list, taken from four different albums.

10. Heavyweights
The following bands are obviously very well known. But what might have escaped casual fans of our favorite genre is that these classic bands have pretty great post-2000 catalogs. If you loved these guys in the late 80s, definitely take the time to check out their recent work. You might be surprised

at how much quality these bands have released: Whitesnake – give a listen to *Good to be Bad* and *Forever More*; Europe – *Last Look at Eden, Start From the Dark* and *War of Kings*; Kingdom Come – *Ain't Crying For the Moon, Rendered Waters* and *Too*; and Great White – *Elated, Back to the Rhythm* and *Rising*.

This next list is more of what would be referred to as the deep cuts of a classic album! Below are bands that had that one killer album, and then maybe one or two more outputs that didn't do much on the rock charts. Some of the names you might recognize, others you might not. Either way they have a lot to offer to your iPod's music selection.

We hate it when a publication runs a "Best Unknown Hair Bands" list and the story features extremely well know bands like Faster Pussycat and Danger Danger. Below is a more accurate representation of what the real answers should be.

You've listened to the entire catalog of all the major bands from the 80s and early 90s and are looking for something you might have missed? Check out the following list.

Slik Toxic
Do you love Skid Row and Motley Crue? If so, you must stop everything you are doing and immediately listen to Slik Toxic's *Doin' the Nasty*. We love this album so much we've ranked it as one of the 30 best albums ever released in the HM/HB genre.

Salty Dog
If Guns N' Roses is your band, then along with owning everything by Dangerous Toys you must also purchase *Every Dog Has its Day* by Salty Dog. The rasp is on point, especially on songs like Come Along, Sacrifice Me and Just Like a Woman.

Wildside

They were supposed to be the Hair Metal's next big thing. Unfortunately, they put out their debut album a couple years too late. But luckily for us, you can still slap *Under the Influence* into your CD player today and rock out like it was still 1987!!! Guitar player Brent Woods was taught by legendary Randy Rhoads and currently shreds for Sebastian Bach's solo band.

KINGOFTHEHILL
Frankie Muriel is one of the best entertainers/performers in the history of the HM/HB genre. And the dude still sounds amazing today. They released two fantastic albums. Their self-titled debut in 1991 and then the follow-up album, which was written/recorded and then scratched in the early 90s. Luckily for rock fans that album was released in 2005, the aptly titled *Unreleased*. Buy them both and thank us later. Funk-rock and great ballads, what more could one want!

Tyketto
How to describe Tyketto? Maybe a heavier version of Bon Jovi. They've released several albums for you to enjoy, but their two best are *Don't Come Easy* from 1991 and *Reach* from 2016! Check out Forever Young and Standing Alone.

D'Molls
D'Molls released two pretty solid albums, *D'Molls* in 1988 and *Warped* in 1990. Listen to All I Want and This Time it's Love to get a feel for the sound of this great band.

Alleycat Scratch
Deadboys in Trash City, released in 1993, produced the amazing ballad Roses on Your Grave.

Hericane Alice

Only one album, but what a great one it was! Bruce Naumann could hit the high notes like nobody's business. The album is called *Tear Down the House*. Great songs include Dream Girl, Too Late and Wild, Young and Crazy.

Wild Boyz
Willie D had such a great and unique voice for the Wild Boyz, who released the fantastic 1991 album *Unleashed*. Check out Roll the Dice for a cool rocker, I Don't Wanna Cry No More for a pop hit and to hear one of the highest notes ever sang in the genre, take a listen to power ballad Forever.

Wig Wam
Norwegian band Wig Wam hung up their instruments in 2014. But before that they released four really quality glam Hair Band albums. Wig Wam has nine songs in our Top 1,000 list – led by Mine all Mine and Tell Me Where To Go.

Deaf Dumb & Blond
DD&B released *L.A. Days* in 2017, but the songs come from their Sunset Strip days in the early 90s. The album will also take you back to those days. Plop in *L.A. Days* and you'll feel like it's 1991 all over again.

Shanghai
Two great albums from the early 1990s – *Take Another Bite* and *Bombs Away*. The real highlight from the band is Love Has it's Reasons, which we slotted as the number one power ballad of 2001.

Electric Boys
They had a minor hit in All Lips N' Hips back in 1989, but even though the Electric Boys never really exploded after that, the band has released five pretty solid albums over the last 28 years.

Vains of Jenna
Vains of Jenna had a lot of backing from big name US rockers, including Stevie Rachelle of Tuff, when they broke in the states. Unfortunately, after a couple

killer albums the Swedish based band called it quits. *The Art of Telling Lies* would be their album to check out first. They have four songs in our Top 1,000.

Bad City
One album wonders, Chicago based Bad City's *Welcome to the Wasteland* is a fantastic disc of music. Buy it and rock out to their unique and full sound. For a quick taste, listen to Touch and Fire in the Pouring Rain.

Big Cock
Ignore the name and enjoy Robert Mason's side project. Four great albums. Think of a heavier and more original version of Steel Panther.

Joey C. Jones
Just one album and it was released 25 years after most of it was written, but wow, what an album it was. Vocalist Joey Jones really shines on Summer Song and Picture Yourself, two songs that made the top 150 of our Top 1,000 list. The album is called *Melodies for the Masses*. You should own it.

Underrated SONGS:

Below is our list of songs that we felt should have been bigger, more popular and consider staples of the hair metal genre. For whatever reasons fans didn't really connect to these badass rockers like they should have. You might think you've heard anything and everything released from The Day. We urge you to carve out an hour of time, grab a drink, turn the lights off, turn the volume up to 10……and enjoy these underrated masterpieces.

1. **Angel N U - Dangerous Toys (Hellacious Acres)**

Anybody who doesn't list Dangerous Toys as one of the top hair metal bands of all time needs to relinquish their metal card. Angel N U is unlike anything released in the late 80s or early 90s. It's a shame this song didn't blow up. This seven-minute rocker has one of the best grooves from any song of the era. And the guitar work kicks major ass as well.

2. Face – Warrant (Under the Influence)
The last song recorded and released by the ultra-talented Jani Lane with Warrant.
Face shows just how much Lane had grown as a songwriter and vocalist. Face rises above anthems like Cherry Pie and Down Boys and just shows how brilliant the rest of Lane's career should have/could have been. Face was co-written by guitar player Keri Kelli.

3. Summer Song – Joey C. Jones (Melodies for the Masses)
The song that the should-have-been superstar Joey C. Jones used to close shows with during the early days. Luckily Jones released a quality studio version of this hair metal classic on his greatest hits album. Why Summer Song wasn't a top 40 hit is a crime.

4. Sweet Asylum - Slik Toxic (Doin' the Nasty)
Helluvatime was the Canadian band's big hit in 1992, but Sweet Asylum was the best song on the their debut album - Doin' the Nasty. Nick Walsh's vocals rival Sebastian Bach's range. Great band that didn't get the US exposure/recognition that they deserved.

5. Time To Let You Go - Enuff Z'Nuff (Strength)
Enuff Z'Nuff were often compared to The Beatles back in the day. I actually thought Time To Let You Go was a Beatle's cover the a couple years – that's how good this song is. Enuff Z'Nuff at its finest.

6. These Days - Bon Jovi (These Days)
The last great Bon Jovi song released on the last great Bon Jovi album: These

Days, released in 1996. A darker, heavier, more mature Bon Jovi - gotta love it. Really wish the band would go back to this sound rather than the country-pop stuff they are releasing now.

7. Bang Goes The Bell - Babylon A.D. (Babylon A.D.)
Bang, released in 1989, is hard, catchy and a tune you can't keep out of your head. Great song, great band, great singer. Derek Davis still sounds amazing today.

8. Cold Blood – Kix (Blow My Fuse)
Cold Blood was a modest hit for Kix, so one might think it doesn't deserve a spot on this list. BUT this is one of the few hair metal era songs that actually has not only stood the test of time, but sounds better today than it did 25 years ago. I dare you to crank this song up on your stereo and not throw your fists in the air!

9. Caught in a Dream – Tesla (Into the Now)
The ten year wait between albums was almost worth it simply because of the brilliant Caught in a Dream, which is Tesla's last great song. Released in 2004 Caught in a Dream sounds like classic Tesla and like it could have been right off of Bust a Nut or Psychotic Supper.

10. Queen of the Nile - Dangerous Toys (Dangerous Toys)
Two songs in the top 10? Yes, Dangerous Toys were that good. And unfortunately - that underrated. DT's greatest hits really stacks up well against the heavyweight bands of the era. They were a step above the majority of the hair metal staple bands.
Queen of the Nile is the band's You Could Be Mine. Just a great hard rocking song off their self titled 1989 release. Jason McMaster's voice really shines on Queen.

11. Let It Go – Def Leppard (High 'n' Dry)
You can literally hear 10 different bands entire catalog in this song.

12. If I Die Tomorrow - Motley Crue (Red, White and Crue)
In 2005 Motley Crue turned a song written by Simple Plan into a huge rock hit.

13. Walking Shoes - Tora Tora
1989 saw the best blues based rock band of the hair metal era releasing the classic Surprise Attack. Anthony Corder's voice still blows me away.

14. Shelter Me – Cinderella (Heartbreak Station)
In our opinion, Cinderella's best overall song.

15.   Mother Blues – Arcade (Arcade)
Stephen Pearcy leaves Ratt and releases the most interesting song of his career.

16.   Your Momma Won't Know - Pretty Boy Floyd (Leather Boyz with Electric Toys)
Way better song, way better lyrics than I Wanna Be With You.

17. Roll The Dice – Wild Boyz (Unleashed)
Willie D and the boys released a classic album in 1989. Check out the ballad Forever as well. Willie hits a high note that would make Rob Halford jealous.

18. Hollywood – Junkyard (Junkyard)
Sleaze rock at its finest, just as good as their hit Simple Man.

19. Yesterdays – GnR (Use Your Illusions II)
Lost in the shuffle from all the singles and videos from the 1991 Illusions - Yesterdays is Axl at his mellow finest. A stripped down melodic rocker with great lyrics. Brilliant song.

20. I Do You - KINGOFTHEHILL
1991 featured the funkiest rock band alive - KINGOFTHEHILL. Also check out

If I Say, a fantastic power ballad.

21. Someone Special - Hardcore Superstar (Bad Sneakers and a Pina Colada)
In our opinions, the greatest hard rock band alive right now out there touring. Someone Special is their anthem.

22. Sad Theresa – Warrant (Dog Eat Dog)
Hair metal was dying out to grunge, but Warrant did their best to keep our favorite genre alive with the amazing album *Dog Eat Dog*. So many great songs on it, but Sad Theresa is the best.

23. Laugh 'n' a ½ D.A.D. (Riskin' It All)
Do these guys ever put out a bad song? Jesper Binzer's vocals really shine.

24. Shake & Tumble – FireHouse (FireHouse)
Don't Treat Me Bad was the hit….but Shake & Tumble is FireHouse's coolest song.

25. Days Gone Bye – Slaughter (The Wild Life)
The best song from the 1992 release. Mark Slaughter releases a heavier version than most power ballads. And that's a great thing for fans.

26. Little Fighter - White Lion (Big Game)
Mike Tramp has never received the credit he deserves for his brilliant song-writing skills.

27. Civil War - Guns n Roses (Use Your Illusion II)
Slash wrote the music and Axl Rose tacked on the riveting lyrics in what is probably Guns N Roses most intelligent and adult song

28. Screamin' For More - Dangerous Toys (Pissed)

We love it, mostly because it doesn't sound like every other hair metal song ever released. Dangerous Toys changed their sound up a bit – and it worked, big time.

29. Stained Glass Heart - Michael Monroe (Horns and Halos)
Brilliant solo song released from the ex-Hanoi Rocks singer.

30. Far Away – Shameless (Queen For a Day)
One of the best power ballads of all time. Steve Summers really shines.

31. Driftaway – Motley Crue (Motley Crue)
The best song the band recorded with John Corabi. The second half of the song is off the charts great.

32. By Your Side – Sebastian Bach (Angel Down)
Bach's best ballad post Skid Row. Feel free to check out Breakin' Down, another underrated ballad by Baz/Skid Row.

33/34. Try So Hard/Stir It Up - Tesla
I went back and forth a hundred times on which song to rank higher, so I finally decided to just combine these two amazing Tesla songs. Tesla's deeper cuts are often stronger songs than the popular "hits" that everybody knows. Try So Hard is from 1994's Bust a Nut. Stir It Up comes from the 1991 album Psychotic Supper. Two amazing songs.

35. Mr. Rainmaker – Warrant (Cherry Pie)
The second catchiest song off of 1990's Cherry Pie. Should have been a single and a hit.

36-39. Street of Dreams/Better/TWAT/Catcher – GnR (Chinese Democracy)
The four best songs of the super underrated album from Axl Rose's Guns N' Roses in 2008.

40. **Dreamtime – L.A. Guns (Shrinking Violet)**
Jizzy Pearl's best song with L.A. Guns.

BILLBOARD CHARTS
(Information taken from Billboard.com. Unfortunately, we did find a couple mistakes while researching. For example, a song might have been listed at reaching #4 during a specific week's chart…but then in the overall section for that band, it would say the song reached #8. And then on the band's Wiki page or official website, it might say the same song reached #2. We tried our best to research and be as accurate as possible).

Billboard Top 200 Album Chart
Albums that reached number one

Appetite for Destruction – Guns N' Roses: 172 weeks (1987)

Hysteria – Def Leppard: 133 weeks (1987)

Slippery When Wet – Bon Jovi: 118 weeks (1986)

Use Your Illusion II – Guns N' Roses: 106 weeks (1991)

Metal Health – Quiet Riot (1983)
New Jersey – Bon Jovi (1988)
Dr. Feelgood - Motley Crue (1989)
Slave to the Grind – Skid Row (1991)
Adrenalize – Def Leppard (1992)
Lost Highway – Bon Jovi (2007)
The Circle - Bon Jovi (2009)
What About Now - Bon Jovi (2013)
This House is Not For Sale – Bon Jovi (2016)

Albums that peaked at number two
Pyromania – Def Leppard (1983)
Girls, Girls, Girls – Motley Crue (1987)
Whitesnake - Whitesnake (1987)
Open Up and Say Ah – Poison (1988)
Lies – Guns N' Roses (1988)
Use Your Illusion I – Guns N' Roses (1991)
Decade of Decadence – Motley Crue (1991)
Bounce – Bon Jovi (2002)
Have a Nice Day – Bon Jovi (2005)

Albums that peaked at number three
Night Songs - Cinderella (1987)
Greatest Hits – Guns N' Roses (2004)
Chinese Democracy – Guns N' Roses (2008)

Albums that peaked at number four
Spaghetti Incident – Guns N' Roses (1993)
Generation Swine – Motley Crue (1997)
Saints of Los Angeles – Motley Crue (2008)

Albums that peaked at number five
Keep The Faith – Bon Jovi (1992)
Songs from Sparkle Lounge – Def Leppard (2008)
Ultimate Collection – Bon Jovi (2010)

SIX
Theatre Of Pain – Motley Crue (1985)
Skid Row – Skid Row (1989)
Red, White & Crue – Motley Crue (2005)

SEVEN
Out of the Cellar - Ratt (1984)
Invasion of Privacy - Ratt (1985)

Cherry Pie – Warrant (1990)
Motley Crue – Motley Crue (1994)
EIGHT
The Final Countdown – Europe (1987)
The Wild Life - Slaughter (1992)
Cross Road – Bon Jovi (1994)

NINE
Twice Shy – Great White (1989)
Retro Active – Def Leppard (1993)
These Days – Bon Jovi (1995)
Crush, - Bon Jovi (2000)
TEN
Long Cold Winter – Cinderella (1988)
Slip Of the Tongue - Whitesnake (1989)
Dirty Rotten Filthy Stinking Rich - Warrant (1989)
Rock of Ages – Def Leppard (2005)
Def Leppard – Def Leppard (2015)
11-15
Pride - White Lion
Euphoria – Def Leppard
X – Def Leppard
Five Man Acoustical Jam - Tesla
Kingdom Come – Kingdom Come
Back For the Attack – Dokken
Burning Bridges – Bon Jovi
Psychotic Supper – Tesla
Exposed – Vince Neil
Slang – Def Leppard
This Left Feels Right – Bon Jovi
Vault – Def Leppard
Conditional Critical – Quiet Riot

Stay Hungry – Twisted Sister
In the Heart of the Young - Winger
Lean Into It – Mr. Big

16-20

Yeah! – Def Leppard
Mirror Ball, Live & More – Def Leppard
Shout At the Devil – Motley Crue
Reach For the Sky - Ratt
Hooked – Great White
The Great Radio Controversy - Tesla
Stick it To Ya - Slaughter
Out of This World - Europe
Big Game - White Lion
Heartbreak Station - Cinderella
Greatest Hits – Motley Crue
One Wild Night – Bon Jovi
Bust A Nut - Tesla

21-29

Winger - Winger
Once Bitten - Great White
Detonator - Ratt
Simplicity - Tesla
Viva! Hysteria – Def Leppard
Dog Eat Dog – Def Leppard
Dancing Undercover - Ratt
Trixter - Trixter
Lita - Lita Ford
Zebra - Zebra

30-39

Infestation - Ratt
Fastway - Fastway
Into The Now - Tesla
Under Lock and Key – Dokken

In God We Trust - Stryper
To Hell With The Devil - Stryper
Mechanical Resonance - Tesla
Forever More - Tesla
Beast From the East – Dokken
No More Hell To Pay - Stryper
Subhuman Race - Skid Row
Cocked and Loaded – LA Guns
Against The Law - Stryper
7800 Degrees Fahrenheit – Bon Jovi
The Disregard of Timekeeping - Bonham
High N Dry - Def Leppard
Britny Fox – Britny Fox

Hot 100 Singles

Reached Number One
Love Bites – Def Leppard (1987)
Here I Go Again – Whitesnake (1987)
I'll Be There For You – Bon Jovi (1989)
Bad Medicine – Bon Jovi (1988)
Livin' On a Prayer - Bon Jovi (1987)
You Give Love a Bad Name – Bon Jovi (1986)
Sweet Child O' Mine – Guns N' Roses (1988)
To Be With You – Mr. Big (1992)
Every Rose Has Its Thorn – Poison (1988)

Peaked at number two
Pour Some Sugar On Me – Def Leppard (1987)
Is This Love – Whitesnake (1987)
Heaven – Warrant (1989)
Peaked at number three

Armageddon It – Def Leppard (1988)
Born To Be My Baby – Bon Jovi (1989)
Carrie – Europe (1987)
When the Children Cry – White Lion (1989)
November Rain – Guns N' Roses (1992)
Unskinny Bop – Poison (1990)
Peaked at number four
Always – Bon Jovi (1994)
Patience – Guns N' Roses (1989)
18 and Life – Skid Row (1989)
Something To Believe In - Poison (1990)
Peaked at number five
Once Bitten, Twice Shy – Great White (1989)
Cum On Feel The Noize – Quiet Riot (1983)
Paradise City – Guns N' Roses (1989)
Love of a Lifetime – FireHouse (1991)
SIX
Dr. Feelgood – Motley Crue (1989)
I Remember You – Skid Row (1990)
Nothing But a Good time – Poison (1988)
SEVEN
Lay Your Hands on Me – Bon Jovi (1989)
Wanted Dead Or Alive – Bon Jovi (1987)
Welcome to the Jungle – Guns N' Roses (1988)
EIGHT
Without You – Motley Crue (1989)
The Final Countdown - Europe (1987)
Close My Eyes Forever - Lita Ford (1988)
Wait - White Lion (1988)
Signs – Tesla (1991)
When I look Into Your Eyes - FireHouse (1992)
NINE
Living In Sin – Bon Jovi (1989)

TEN
Hysteria – Def Leppard (1987)
Bed of Roses – Bon Jovi (1993)
Love Song – Tesla (1990)
Don't Cry – Guns N' Roses (1991)
I Saw Red - Warrant (1991)
Cherry Pie - Warrant (1990)
You're Momma Don't Dance – Poison (1988)
11-15
Don't Close Your Eyes – Kix
Rocket – Def Leppard
Photograph – Def Leppard
Two Steps Behind – Def Leppard
Girls, Girls, Girls – Motley Crue
Round and Round - Ratt
Kiss Me Deadly – Lita Ford
Don't Know What You Got - Cinderella
Miles Away – Winger
Love Is On The Way - Saigon Kick
Have You Ever Needed Somebody So Bad – Def Leppard
Fallen Angel - Poison
Nobody's Fool - Cinderella
This Ain't a Love Song – Bon Jovi
Lets Get Rocked – Def Leppard
16-20
Rock of Ages – Def Leppard
Home Sweet Home – Motley Crue
Just Take My Heart – Mr. Big
Animal – Def Leppard
Don't Go Away Mad – Motley Crue
Headed For a Heartbreak - Winger
Fly To the Angels - Slaughter
Don't Treat Me Bad - Firehouse

Coming Home - Cinderella
Sometimes She Cries - Warrant
21-30
Were Not Gonna Take It – Twisted Sister
Cryin' – Vixen
Who Says You Can't Go Home – Bon Jovi
Honestly - Stryper
I'll Never Let You Go - Steelheart
Seventeen - Winger
Edge of a Broken Heart - Vixen
I Live My Life For You - Firehouse
Kickstart My Heart – Bon Jovi
Make a Memory – Bon Jovi
In These Arms – Bon Jovi
Down Boys - Warrant
Wild World – Mr. Big
Up All Night - Slaughter
Foolin' – Def Leppard
The Deeper The Love - Whitesnake
House of Pain – Faster Pussycat
Keep The Faith – Bon Jovi
You Could Be Mine – Guns N' Roses
The Angel Song – Great White
Rock The Night - Europe
31-40
Metal Health – Quiet Riot
Superstitious - Europe
It's My Life – Bon Jovi
The Ballad of Jayne – L.A. Guns
Live and Let Die – Guns N' Roses
Stand Up and Kick Love Into Motion – Def Leppard
Chinese Democracy – Guns N' Roses
Life Goes On - Poison

Shelter Me – Cinderella
The Last Mile – Cinderella
Make Love Like a Man – Def Leppard
Fool For Your Loving - Whitesnake
Ride the Wind - Poison
Runaway – Bon Jovi
Miss You In a Heartbeat – Def Leppard
Spend My Life - Slaughter
Lay it Down - Ratt

Billboard Rock Chart
ONE
Photograph – Def Leppard
Rock of Ages – Def Leppard
Lets Get Rocked – Def Leppard
Stand Up and Kick Love into Motion – Def Leppard
Keep The Faith – Bon Jovi
Living On a Prayer – Bon Jovi
Promises – Def Leppard
TWO
Fool For Your Loving - Whitensake
Signs - Tesla
THREE
Make Love Like a Man – Def Leppard
Love Bites – Def Leppard
Armageddon – Def Leppard
Bad Medicine – Bon Jovi
Don't Cry – Guns N' Roses
You Could Be Mine – Guns N' Roses
Heaven – Warrant

Current Bands Kicking Ass

The one question we get asked more than any other is "are there any bands out there today that are putting out kick ass 80s hair metal music?" The answer is simple. Why yes, as a matter of fact, there are a bunch of them!!!

Below is a list of the bands that are currently keeping the Hair Metal genre alive. Bands that would have been perfect compliments to the scene if they would have been releasing albums in 1989! Don't let anybody tell you that rock is dead. These bands prove that the HM/HB genre is still alive and kicking.

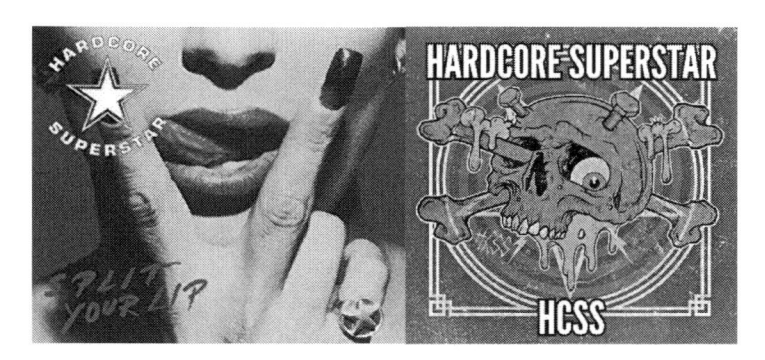

1. Hardcore Superstar

The cream of the crop is Sweden's Hardcore Superstar. Joakim Berg is an absolute beast and is easily the best modern rock singer alive today.

If you enjoy the hard rock aspect of the HM/HB gene, Hardcore Superstar is the band for you. Parts Guns N' Roses, AC/DC, Van Halen with a little bit of Motley Crue and Skid Row mixed in. If Hardcore Superstar had started their career in 1986 we have no doubt they'd be ranked as one of the top 20 hair metal bands of all time.

Arena rockers, metal mayhem, power ballads, punk, and hard rock – HCSS nails them all.

They've put out 10 albums since their debut in 1998. Twenty-six songs from those albums grace our Top 1,000 songs list. Want an old school hard rock band? Go buy every HCSS album and you'll be set for the next year.

Best album: It's Only Rock 'n' Roll
Key Songs: Someone Special, Dreamin' in a Casket, Long Time No See

https://www.facebook.com/OfficialHardcoreSuperstar
https://twitter.com/hcssofficial

2. Shameless

If you love the glam rock side of HM/HB music, then Shameless is a delightful treat of a band. The fact that Shameless isn't more recognized as an upper tier band right now is beyond us.

Shameless has been a bit of an all-star band in the past, but currently Tuff's Stevie Rachelle and Pretty Boy Floyd's Steve Summers are handling the majority of the vocals. All-stars that have played with Shameless include Tracii Guns, Bruce Kulick, Jani Lane and Robert Sweet.

Alexx Michael started and runs the band.

Shameless has 11 songs on our top 1,000 list and four albums in our top albums list.

Best Album: Famous 4 Madness
Key Songs: Far Away, She's Not Coming Home Tonight, Better Off Without You

http://shamelessrock.com/
https://www.facebook.com/Shamelessrock

3. Reckless Love

Finish based Reckless Love is one of the most successful bands on the list. We Are the Weekend and Reckless Love highlight a list of 11 songs that made our Top 1,000 chart.

All four of their albums made our albums list as well.

Best Album: Animal Attraction
Key Songs: We Are the Weekend, Hot Rain, Night on Fire

https://www.facebook.com/RecklessLove

4. The Last Vegas

One of the best American-based hard rock bands out there right now is The Last Vegas. They've released seven albums since 2004, including three that landed in our top 350 albums list.

The power ballad Apologize is one of the best hard rock power ballads of all time.

Best Album: Eat Me
Key Songs: Apologize, Hard to Get Over You, Evil Eyes

http://thelastvegas.com/
https://www.facebook.com/thelastvegas

5. Crashdiet

The Swedish rockers have released four albums, two that are really great. Simon Cruz fronted the band for a bit. Their 2017 album featured the band's fourth lead singer. Check out *Rest in Sleaze* and *Generation Wild*.

They have six songs in our Top 1,000 list.

Best Album: Rest in Sleaze
Key Songs: Save Her, Beautiful Pain, It's a Miracle

http://www.crashdiet.org/
https://www.facebook.com/crashdietband/

6. Santa Cruz

They've only released three albums, but Finnish band Santa Cruz has made their mark on the American hair metal audience. Bits of their songs have been featured in major TV commercials and on ESPN highlight clips. We Are the Ones to Fall is the highlight song. The band has six tunes in our top 1,000.

Best Album: Santa Cruz
Key Songs: We Are the Ones to Fall, Get Me Out of California, Aiming High

http://santacruzbandofficial.com/resurrection/
https://www.facebook.com/santacruzband

7. Crazy Lixx

With six albums in the last ten years, the Swedish band Crazy Lixx is carrying on the HM/HB torch with music that some compare to Def Leppard and Motley Crue! That might be a stretch, but Crazy Lixx does kick some serious ass. They've got eight songs in our top 1,000. Listen to What of Our Love and Heroes are Forever.

Best Album: New Religion
Key Songs: What of Our Love, Heroes Are Forever, Outlaw

https://www.crazylixx.com/
https://www.facebook.com/crazylixx

8. Hell in the Club

Italy is represented with the amazing band Hell in the Club. They've got four songs that made our yearly top songs lists.

Best Album: Let the Games Begin
Key Songs: Naked, The Life & Death of Mr. Nobody, Star

http://www.hellintheclub.com/
https://www.facebook.com/hellintheclub

9. Babylon Bombs

Swedish rockers Babylon Bombs turned in the top power ballad of 2006. They've released four major albums – all of them are great.

Best Album: Babylon's Burning
Key Songs: Slip Away, It's Alright, Babylon's Burning

http://babylonbombs.net/
https://www.facebook.com/babylonbombs

10. Tales From the Porn

Tuff singer Stevie Rachelle has teamed up with Brazilian based Tales From the Porn to release one of the 2017's best albums: *H.M.M.V.*

Best Album: H.M.M.V.
Key Songs: Girls Want to Party, Perfect Love

https://www.facebook.com/talesfromtheporn/
https://twitter.com/tftp_official

Others:
Other bands of note. Some are current, some are semi-active, some are lessor known 80's bands that are still releasing albums today.

Hannon Tramp: Their self-titled album was released in 2014, but full of songs written in the 1980s. Hopefully these guys will continue writing and recording. How Many Times is our choice for best power ballad of 2014.

Stage Dolls: Melodic rock band Stage Dolls have been releasing albums since 1985. But our favorite would be 2004's *Get a Life*. Hard To Say Goodbye is their signature ballad.

Darkhorse: Paule Laine delivers the goods with his album *Let it Ride*. Strong and Better Days are the key tracks.

Beggars and Thieves: They've released five albums since 1990. Four of their songs landed in our top 1,000 list. What's Going On and Kill Me are their top rated tunes.

Steel Panther: Love them or hate them, we have to list Michael Starr and company on our list. While they produce "joke" type songs, nobody can deny how individually talented the band members are.

Vains of Jenna: Sweden-based sleaze metal band, managed by Tuff's Stevie Rachelle. Lit Up/Let Down is their signature album. Best songs are Paper Heart and Set it Off. They had the potential to be huge!

Private Line: Finland's Private Line have released three really great albums. Start off with 2004's 21st Century Pirates and the songs Bleed and Selflove-Sick.

Wig Wam: Norwegian rockers Wig Wam called it a quit a couple years ago, but not before releasing four great albums between 2004-2012. Wig Wamania is the best album, Mine All Mine and Tell Me Where To Go are two of the top songs. Lead singer Age Sten Nilsen has a new band – Ammunition – that kicks a lot of ass.

Love Razer:
Canada's hottest young hair metal band! They started as an 80s tribute band and had so much fun – as well as talent – they started writing their own material and turned into a kick-ass band that's keeping the hair metal spirit alive.

Once you get through those band's catalogs, be sure and check out: Kickin Valentina, The Wild, The Darkness (some people love them, some can't stand them), Toyko Motor Fist (or anything from legendary Ted Poley), Biters, Confess, The Defiants, The Dead Daisies, Sons of Apollo, Niterain, Tyketto, Tigertailz.

DUDES WHO DESERVE MORE CREDIT

While lead singers get all the glory and adoration, below we've listed band members that have been instrumental to their band's success. Some have received more recognition than others, but this is the list of the dudes who were the real heart and soul of their bands.

Slash and Izzy - Guns N' Roses

It's hard to make your mark when the most high profile singer in the business - Axl Rose – fronts your band. But for Guns N' Roses, there is no denying the important of guitar players Slash and Izzy Stradlin.

Slash is obviously recognized as a guitar God not just in the hair metal genre, but in relation to all guitar players in rock history. He has written and shared numerous iconic guitar riffs and solos, while also co-writing several GnR classics like "You're Crazy", "Civil War", "Coma" and "Perfect Crime."

Izzy is a decent guitar player, but his main contribution to GnR comes from his impressive song-writing skills. Stradlin wrote or is listed as a co-writer on more than half of GnR's pre-Chinese Democracy catalog. His biggest hits include "Used to Love Her", "Don't Cry" and "You Could Be Mine".

Paul Gilbert and Billy Sheehan – Mr. Big
Talent wise it doesn't get much better than Mr. Big's Gilbert and Sheehan. Gilbert is a guitar virtuoso, easily one of the five best players in the genre. He co-wrote about half of Mr. Big's catalog, including being the sole writer of the great song "Green Tinted Sixties Minds".

Sheehan is also one of the best bass players in HM/HB genre's history. Like Gilbert, he also is listed as co-writer on about half of Mr. Big's song catalog.

Nikki Sixx – Motley Crue
Sixx is obviously one of the most well known figures in Hair Metal history. But the remarkable part is that his bass playing is the lowest ranked part of his legendary status.

Sixx wrote or co-wrote all of Motley's catalog. He has essentially been the band's agent, promoter, manager, public relations agent, etc. Sixx is essentially the engine that drove Motley Crue to worldwide success. Without Sixx there wouldn't have been a Motley Crue.

DiMartini/Crosby
Stephen Pearcy has that mistakable voice. But many think the real heart and soul of Ratt was the guitar duo of Warren DeMartini and Robbin Crosby. DiMartini is a monster on the guitar, one of the best shredders of the genre. Crosby teamed up with DiMartini to give Ratt a potent guitar-attack, as he was also an upper tier lead player.

The Ratt duo were also proficient writers. The two have co-writing credits on the majority of Ratt's songs – especially all the hits. Crosby on "Round and Round", "Wanted Man", "Lay it Down" and "Body Talk". DiMartini also on "Round and Round" and "Lay it Down" as well as "Slip of the Lip", "Way Cool Jr." and "Loving You's a Dirty Job".

Donnie Purnell
Purnell was the main songwriter for Kix until his falling out with the band in the mid-90s. Bass player Purnell wrote or co-wrote all of the band's hits, including Blow My Fuse, Cold Blood and Don't Close Your Eyes.

Purnell also co-produced the band's most successful album – Blow My Fuse.

Steve Clark
A lot of fans feel like Def Leppard lost their balls as a hard rock band after guitar player Clark passed away.

Clark was an amazing guitar player, able to effortlessly switch back from being lead or rhythm. Clark was also an excellent songwriter, sharing co-writing credits on 90% of all Def Leppard songs through the *Hysteria* album, including all the band's major hits.

Bolan and Sabo
Sebastian Bach has that magical voice. But the guys who wrote the songs that propelled Skid Row to stardom were bass player Rachel Bolan and guitar player Dave Sabo.

Bolan wrote or co-wrote virtually every Skid Row song, including all the classics: "Youth Gone Wild", "I Remember You", "Monkey Business" and "18 and Life". Bolan, along with being an accomplished musician and writer, has also produced several songs and albums for other bands. Sabo doesn't have quite the same number as writing credits as Bolan, but he does own the sole writing credit on "Breakin' Down", which is the best Skid Row song released since the band's *Slave to the Grind* album.

Fred Coury
Coury is the top-ranked drummer on the list. While most known for his drumming and producing skills with Cinderella, Coury has also played with Guns N' Roses and Night Ranger, as well as produced songs and albums for numerous other bands.

Coury is also an award-winning composure, scoring for TV series like The Night Shift and The Wall.

Mark Kendall
Kendall has done it all for Great White. He helped start the band, has co-wrote the majority of their songs, co-produce the *Once Bitten* album and is a top-notch guitar player.

Dana Strum
While not being the most liked musician in the genre, bass player Strum has had a remarkable career. In his early days, he has been credited with introducing both Randy Rhoads and Jake E Lee to Ozzy.

Strum then joined the Vinnie Vincent Invasion and was listed as co-producer for both the band's albums. Joined Mark Slaughter in the band Slaughter, and was a co-writer on 100% of the band's first three albums, which he also co-produced.

Strum has also played with the Vince Neil band, as well as producing albums for other artists, most notably Kik Tracee's 1991 *No Rules*.

Gilby Clarke
To a lot of people, Gilby is that dude who replaced Izzy Stradlin in GnR. But for those of us in the know, the GnR gig was just 1% of Clarke's career!

Gilby's resume is extremely impressive. He has played with, worked with or produced albums/songs with: Guns N' Roses, Heart, Slash's Snakepit, Nancy Sinatra, LA Guns and virtually ever other hair metal star from the late 80s and early 90s.

Honorable Mention:

George Lynch: legendary guitar player and co-wrote a lot of Dokken's discography. Also the driving force behind the critically acclaimed Lynch Mob.

Jeff Pilson: Co-wrote almost every song for Dokken. Wrote "Dream Warriors" with George Lynch. Great backup singer, great piano player, and played acoustic guitar on some Dokken songs.

Frank Hannon: phenomenal guitar player, co-wrote most of Tesla's popular material.

John Sykes: Writing credits on almost every song of Whitesnake's 1987 signature album. Also wrote, produced and played lead guitar on three blue Murder albums. Very underrated talent.

Richie Sambora: Bon Jovi was more than just their lead singer. Sambora is a well-respected guitar player, but he also co-wrote and helped produced a number of Bon Jovi legendary songs and albums. Had three solo albums that he wrote and produced.

Reb Beach: extremely versatile guitar player. There is a reason that he has been chosen to play with Winger, Dokken. Danger Danger and Whitesnake, Twisted Sister as well as Fiona and The Bee Gees.

Keri Kelli: Dude has played in more well known bands than anybody in the genre. Has played with: Pretty Boy Floyd, Slash's Snakepit, Shameless, Warrant, Jani Lane solo, L.A. Guns, Big Bang Babies, Alice Cooper, Adler's Appetite, Stephen Pearcy solo, Tuff and Night Ranger.

Bruno Ravel/Steve West: wrote almost all of Danger Danger's songs. Both have producing credits as well as being very talented musicians. And for fun, they also sang backup vocals on

INTERVIEWS

Chad Cherry
Vocalist of The Last Vegas

Photo courtesy of the The Last Vegas official Facebook page.

1. If you were putting on a horror movie festival, with Alice Cooper closing the festival by playing the entire Along Came a Spider album, what 5-6 movies would you choose to play?

Cherry: We would have to screen all horror movies that The Coop was in or had music on the soundtrack.
1. Monster Dog
2. Nightmare on Elm Street: Freddy's Dead
3. Suck
4. Friday The 13th part 6: Jason Lives
5. Prince Of Darkness

2. We put together a top 1,000 songs of all time list and we have Apologize as the 25th best ballad of the 1981-2017 sleaze metal ear. Thoughts on that?

Cherry: My thoughts are just one question – why isn't Apologize number one?

3. We do have it as the number one ballad of the new era – 2000-through-2017. Can you share with us the story behind Apologize? Was it written about a real relationship?

Cherry: Apologize was originally titled "Dead Roses." Under the production of Nikki Sixx, Marti Frederiksen and TLV we rearranged it in Marti's studio in Burbank to what is now Apologize. It's a scripted song that I think reaches anyone that feels the burden of love and life. It's still the deepest song I've done so far.

4. We also have a section about the "new" era (which is a bit old now, post 2000), but it's basically what new bands to follow today – that sound like the bands we grew up loving (GnR, Crue, Van Halen, etc). We've got you guys as the 4th best current rock band. Does that sound about right to you?

Cherry: Again. Why not number one?

(Editor's Note – the "why not number one" comments were followed with a smile/wink icon)

5. Here is our ranking. Are you fans of any of the bands on the list?
Hardcore Superstar
Shameless
Reckless Love
You Guys
Crashdiet
Santa Cruz
Crazy Lixx
Hell in the Club
Babylon Bombs
Tales From the Porn
Hannon Tramp

Cherry: Jocke from Hardcore Superstar is great. Cool singer and amazing guy. Unfortunately I'm not familiar with any of the other bands. I mostly listen to movie soundtracks and old Rock N Roll. But if you're bringing them up then I'm sure they are all fabulous.

6. All told, you guys have 12 songs in our top 1,000 list, which I think is the second most of anybody that's from the last decade (after Hardcore Superstar). Would you agree with our assessment that you guys and HCSS are the best hard rock bands out there right now?

Cherry: I'm cool with that.

7. Do you he a favorite from your albums or one that really captured the Last Vegas sound the best?

Cherry: I'm a fan of all of our records. Every one of our albums captures our sound. That's kinda the point. I still can't believe we actually recorded all those songs. I hope we can continue creating music while we're still here.

8. How was the rock n' roll scene in Chicago when you were getting started?

Cherry: I would go out when my friends bands were on tour and in town. Music is everywhere in Chicago. Pretty badass. But for the most part I was too busy working on Chad Cherry Clothing to go out.

9. How does a rock band from Chicago name themselves after Vegas?

Cherry: It's a drug reference. I'll let you think about that one.

10. You've worked with both Nikki Sixx and DJ Ashba, who are both legends in the rock world. What's the main thing those two guys taught you?

Cherry: It was an honor and privilege to work with both of them. They taught me the art of fine-tuning a song and how to look deeper into the matter. I've been blessed to be able to work with people that have massive amounts of talent and knowledge.

11. Axl Rose is touring with both the semi-reunion GnR and also with ACDC. With albums reportedly coming from both bands. Which interests you more – a new Guns album or a new ACDC album with Axl on vocals?

Cherry: Both are interesting and cool to me. I dig it.

12. I know you are busy with Claws and The Last Vegas. But is there any other band out there that you would drop everything and go tour with for six months? Maybe an Aerosmith or if Eddie Van Halen called you up?

Cherry: Sure. Only if there's a bowl full of green M&M's at catering every day.

13. If The Last Vegas could tour with any band in 2019 to support a new album, what would your dream bill be?

Cherry: Dr. Teeth and The Electric Mayhem.

14. Everybody knows the story of you guys winning the contest and being signed. But how was your career going before that? How long had the band been together and were you guys out there grinding it out every night?

Cherry: TLV had been on the road basically from 2005- 2008 touring semi successfully and made some die hard underground fans. TLV were on tour when the whole contest dealio happened. We were constantly traveling everywhere playing the coolest rock n roll clubs and making crazy ass fans everywhere we went before Make Rock History happened…which catapulted us forward and more into the lime light.

15. You mentioned in an interview that you liked Cheap Trick. We grew up in rock music, listening to everything. From Metallica to Metal Church to Prince to Buddy Hollyand Chuck Berry to Van Halen and ACDC. But we've never quite understood the love for Cheap Trick (who get tons of love from rockers). What is it about that band that everybody loves?

Cherry: I'm shaking my head at this question.. I'm not sure if I can go on with this interview. How can you be into Buddy Holly and Chuck Berry and not understand Cheap Trick? Jeeeeeeze.

16. You've been the main songwriter for the band. How was it working/writing with Martin Frederiksen.

Cherry: We all write the songs together. Working Marti was incredible. I feel really fortunate to have worked with such a talented and cool guy.

17. At what age did you start singing? And when did you know you were going to sing for a living?

Cherry: I'm not even sure if I know how to sing yet. And I've never made a living from doing it.

18. A lot of bands are touring with just one original member. Would you ever go that route if TLV – keep the band alive, but with a revolving door of musicians? Or do you think there comes a time when a band should retire the name and start fresh with a new name?

Cherry: I really don't care what bands do just at as long as they feel the need to play music and are happy. It's not really any of my business. I don't have the time or energy to teach anybody music from TLV's catalogue. I'd rather stay home and watch Svengoolie.

19. How's the experience been running your own clothes line: Chad Cherry Clothing?

Cherry: The clothing line is a lot of work. I do everything myself and it is all consuming. But I love the fact that people seem to love it as much as my music. I need a clone though, I'm buried in gear.

20. How come you started The Claws? How's that experience been?

Cherry: I live in L.A. Music will find me no matter how much of a recluse I want to be. It's like being in the mob. Once you're in, you're in for life. The Claws catalog of music is growing on a weekly basis. Gary Martin is a seriously strong songwriter and together we come up with my favorite kind of music to play and listen to. And Terry Love is the funkiest bass player out there. I play music with my friends. That's how The Claws started.

21. What does 2018 and 2019 have planned for Chad Cherry, The Last Vegas, The Claws?

Cherry: I'm in the studio recording placement songs for Sony weekly so my vocal chops are better then ever. I'm rehearsing with The Claws once a week, and demo a song with TLV maybe once everything three months plus via cyber space. I really can't predict the future on band stuff. I wish I could tell you there's a 100 new records, song and videos coming out like I usually say in interviews but as of now I'm really not sure. We shall see.

22. Is there anything else you'd like us to mention?

Cherry: Don't forget to take care of each other out there. Love and respect is really what matters, kiddos. Thanks.

https://twitter.com/chad_cherry
https://www.facebook.com/thelastvegas/
http://thelastvegas.com/

Alexx Michael
Shameless

Photo courtesy of Mr. Michael's official Facebook page.

1. How come your initial version of Shameless folded. And then why did you restart the group seven years later?

Michael: The original singer left cause he had a newborn and he moved away from Munich. Musically I was never happy with the original version of the band

2. What were you doing between 1991-1997?

Michael: I did a lot of traveling doing KISS conventions all over the planet and then I hooked up with Eric Singer to start the new version of Shameless.

3. Were you looking at Shameless as a viable band at first (Backstreet Anthems) or more of a collection of All Star talent getting together and doing an album for fun?

Michael: To be honest, I didn't know what to expect. There was no Glam scene at this point and nobody released this kind of music so I thought "lets do it"

Once the album was released the response was so big that pretty much right away I started to work on new songs which turned into the next album *Queen 4 a Day*.

4. How did you get all the stars to work with you? Tell us the story – did you just call all your musician friends and ask them to come jam for a day? Or did you spend hundreds of thousands of dollars to get them to come in? I can't get my friends to come help me cut down a tree in my backyard, but you can get Tracii Guns to come spend days in your studio?

Michael: Eric helped me to get in touch with everybody which helped a lot. When we recorded at Gilby Clarke's place, Tracii came by one day cause he recorded an LA Guns record there as well. He liked the songs and played a few of the leads.

5. Summers/Rachelle would become regulars. But it was cool to see guys like Eddie Robinson and Teddy Andreadis jump on board early on. Alleycat Scratch was great. And Teddy played with GnR – so that's a win-win.

Michael: Eddie was great, but sadly he totally stopped music after this record. He was still so frustrated about Alleycat Scratch so he couldn't motivate himself anymore to do music which I always thought was a big shame cause he was so talented and such a great singer.

5. Gilby Clarke gets a bad rap from the GnR fanbase, but as we researched this project we keep seeing his name over-and-over again for working on and producing albums. What can you say about Mr. Clarke?

Michael: Gilby is such a great and professional guy. He knows everything about guitar sounds and songwriting. Very talented and super nice guy in every way.

6. Queen 4 A Day really announced your guy's presence as being a major

player in the music world. Could you tell while writing it that you had something special?

Michael: I wrote the music for "Queen 4 a Day" already before we did *Backstreet Anthems* and then while I was driving in my car I came up with the chorus. I really felt the song had a great hook and just everything was right about it.

7. You also brought in Keri Kelli, who has literally worked with every hair metal band in the history of the genre. You also had Tracii Guns and Clarke on the album. How do you figure out which musician is going to play on which song? And B.C. doesn't mind all these guitar heroes coming in?

Michael: When I write songs its really easy to know who is the best for which part. BC never had a problem cause he also loved Tracii style.

8. On Splashed, you went with the more solid lineup. How did you choose the guys you wanted for the concrete lineup?

Michael: I just wanted to record in a different way on that record. We spent some great time at Keri's house and then later finished the record in Germany.

9. Going with two singers was a fresh take from the typical band set-up. Do you make Summers and Rachelle arm-wrestle to see who gets what song? How hard is it to schedule Shameless tours when both those guys front other bands?

Michael: It just always comes with the songs. There are certain songs that were better for Stevie and others did fit better for Summers.

10. Who has a better wig – Summers or Bret Michaels?

Michael: Bret Michaels has the worst one in ROCK haha!

11. For Famous 4 Madness you went back to the all-star route with one of your most impressive groups. This time you brought in three great vocalists in Phil Lewis, John Corabi and Lane again. It just boggles my mind that you put together so much talent and produced so many great songs….but Shameless didn't blow up.

Michael: Yeah I know John for a really long time when he was still in Union with Bruce Kulick and Keri did a lot of Work with Phil over time. When I wrote the song "Better Off Without You" I thought it was perfect for Phil and I really liked the idea of having a song were Corabi and Summers would share vocals.

12. Corabi wasn't too heavy for ya'll's sound? How did the collaboration with him come about? Scraggly beard and haired motorcycle driving, raspy vocals, smoking and drinking dude who looks like he could easily kick your ass doesn't seem like a natural selection for a glam band with Steve Summers, who spends 30 minutes making sure his eye shadow matches the color tone of his bandana.

Michael: John is just a great and talented guy and he knew the Shameless stuff for years. He was already supposed to sing a song on *Backstreet Anthems* but he was touring at the time we did the record. This was all before Email and stuff really took off so recording files and sending them somewhere was only possible thru post and that's why we didn't have him on the first album.

13. You literally toured the world to support that album. Is there any country that seems to love you guys more than others? Why do you think you guys aren't more popular in the US? I'd love to see Shameless do the festivals and MORC type shows.

Michael: The problem about the states is just that it's all so huge so its hard where to start and where to go. Plus the competition there is way to big and club tours don't really work anymore in the states for a lot of bands cause the expenses got so high.

14. Too many softball questions. Let's get down to the nitty gritty!!!! Better band: Tuff or Pretty Boy Floyd!!!

Michael: Hard to say. Both have some great material

15. You brought Cherie Currie in for a couple songs off of Beautiful Disaster. Are you a big fan of hers?

Michael: I just thought she would be the perfect voice for the song "Dear Mum" that I wrote

16. You put on a very successful string of Kiss conventions across the world. Have you always been an entrepreneur? Is this your inner-Gene Simmons coming out?

Michael: HAHA maybe one day ;-)

17. Do you think albums will ever make a comeback and be viable again? Fans love to take albums off the Internet for free – but don't realize that they've killed the prospects of their favorite bands releasing music. Will albums ever become viable again? What can rock bands do to make releasing new music a profitable venture again?

Michael: It's not so much what bands can do. It's more the fact that a lot of people got used to getting everything for free these days. Everything is streaming and file sharing these days and people don't see the point of buying music anymore.

18. What did you do when you worked for Apple? Joey Allen of Warrant fame worked Microsoft Certified Professional and worked for a software

company. Did you guys ever randomly cross paths at your non-music job? A music fan would think he was being punked if he was having troubles with his Microsoft Word on his apple computer….and ended up talking to both you and Joey.**

Michael: Haha Yeah I did trainings and workshops for Apple. It was a lot of fun and I learned a lot from it myself.

19. I saw an interview where you made a joke that if you'd grown up on the Sunset Strip you might have spent some time with LA Guns. You know all the main guys from that band. As a musician, can you explain how a legendary band like that become a revolving door of musicians? You had an all star band with guest musicians on several albums and LA Guns still had more members and different line ups than Shameless. Can you explain to the fans, who don't know what goes on behind the scenes, how that ends up happening? It seemed like in the old days, band maintained pretty steady lineups. But today – it's a revolving door of musicians. Money, ego, travel schedules, etc? What causes that?

Michael: Yeah its all of those things pretty much. Music business got really hard over the last 10 years and musicians need to pay the bills as well. Everybody would love to keep a steady line up but its just so hard these days. Back in the days you could play shows pretty much every day of the week. Now it's hard to get people out of their house even during the weekend cause everything is right in front of them on their computer or Phone. They don't need the experience anymore cause they can just see it at home.

20. And are you cool with one original member keeping a band name alive and touring it – even with four brand new members? Or at some point, should a band name be "retired" and a new band started? At some point do you say "Mr. Blotzer, it's you and three brand new guys. Instead of calling yourself Ratt, how about coming up with a new band name."

Michael: I just think it's hard for a lot of musicians to stop their dream and that's why they keep going on. Well Blotzer is different cause he is just an ass. Quiet Riot still sounds great and if you wanna go out and see a live band its perfect. Kevin is dead so to do it like this is the only way. Some people complain about KISS with Tommy & Eric but those people forget about all the younger ones who never saw KISS with Ace & Peter. This way they still can get the experience.

21. Isn't Too Fast For Love really the best overall Motley Crue album?

Michael: Yeah that's true. It's such a great and fresh album. But I also really love *Shout* & *Generation Swine*.

22. Eddie Trunk mentioned that a lot of bands look at fans like cattle, especially during meet-and-greets. Has that been your experience?

Michael: Well Eddie is a bitter KISS fan who cant accept the fact that they won't talk to him anymore since he spends every week bashing the current KISS line up. Sure there are some bands that don't like the contact with their fans but a lot of them know for sure that all they do is only possible because of their fans.

23. Fans are the ones paying a musician's salary (basically) BUT, we can also see how annoying it must be to constantly be harassed by fans every time you are out having lunch or going grocery shopping. "Oh, I love your music. The one song you wrote changed my life. Thank you so much." Jon Bon Jovi has literally heard that same statement 10,000 times. As a celebrity yourself, what advice can you give fans for when they have an interaction with a rock star? Is there something we (fans) can say/do to not be a pain the ass to you?

Michael: I'm a very open person . Just sometimes people can be a nightmare but I don't think of myself as a celebrity. I m just a rock fan who happened to end up on stage haha!

24. Did you really pay $6,000 for for Paul Stanley's boots? Don Dokken is selling his signature hat for $4,500…how high is that on your bucket list?

Michael: Don't know who would buy one of those hats but yeah its almost true. I bought a full Paul Stanley outfit at the official KISS Auction in 2001 but later sold it for way more so it's all good ;-)

25. A common search or question is "are there bands today that sound like the hair bands from the 80s"……so we have a section where we ranked the top 10 bands of the 2000s, that we feel would have been rated right beside the Motley Crue, Cinderella, Guns N' Roses bands if they'd debuted in 1988 instead of the 2000s. Any thoughts on these guys?

Babylon Bombs: Great band with great songs
Hardcore Superstar: I love those guys. I know them for a really long time cause one of my friends did their merch since 1998 or so. They have some amazing songs**.**

26. We've put together a couple different song/album lists. Top 1,000 songs of the entire genre (1981-2017) – broken down between 650 rockers and 350 ballads. And the top 350 album. Shameless scored 11 songs on our top 1,000 list and four albums made the best 350 albums list. Does that seem accurate or a fair representation of your band's success?

Michael: Wow that's awesome. I always love when people are into our music and appreciate the songs I did write

27. The highest-ranking Shameless song is the incredible and amazing ballad Far Away. Thoughts and memories behind that song?

Michael: Aeriel Stiles wrote the song. He wrote almost every Pretty Boy Floyd from the first to the last album. He is such a talented writer but sadly never really got the credit he deserves even everybody loves his songs.

28. Quick Thoughts:

Queen 4 a Day: Still very very proud of this album.
Far Away: Like I said before, amazing song by the one & only Aeriel Stiles
I Don't Think I Love You: Bruce Kulick played such an amazing solo on this track.
Queen 4 a Day: One of those songs that came so easy. Still very proud about it.
She's Not Coming Home Tonight: Once again an amazing song by Aeriel Stiles.
Better Off Without You: I wrote this song when I broke up with this girl. I wrote the song the night before I told her that I can't stay with her anymore.
Famous 4 Madness: Great memories about recording this album.

29. Is there anything at all you would want us to mention or promote?

Michael: At the moment I manage and recorded the new Blue Ruin EP which will be out later this year. I produced the EP together with Anna Monteith who is the drummer and main person of the band. She already did co-write a handful of songs of the last Shameless record "the Filthy 7`. They just shot their first video and will do another one in 2 month before the EP will be released.

Thanks a lot for all the support from friends and fans all over the world. It means the world to me!!!

https://www.facebook.com/weareblueruin/
https://youtu.be/C7tHXhDS1d0
https://www.facebook.com/alexx.michael1
http://shamelessrock.com
https://www.facebook.com/Shamelessrock

HARDCORE SUPERSTAR
The band did a group interview with us. Very friendly guys with a great manager!

1. What is your favorite country to tour? You guys truly do travel the world and play everywhere, which is awesome for the fans. Do you have a couple favorites?

HCSS: It's not easy to pick just a couple but we always love playing Italy as well as the UK, Finland and of course Sweden. We recently played Australia for the first time in 10 years and that was amazing and we loved the last tour we did of the States, especially as we got to play such iconic venues like the Whisky (A Go-Go in Hollywood).

2. How is the hard rock music scene in Sweden?

HCSS: It's fantastic as there are always lots of new bands that are trying to break through, which is healthy as it keeps bands like us on our toes

3. How did you choose to cover "Don't You Ever Leave Me" as you guys do a brilliant job on it. Were you big Hanoi Rocks fans?

HCSS: Of course, we loved Hanoi and especially that song. It was a song that resonated with us, it's a classic that we felt had that Johnny Thunders 'You Can't Put Your Arms Around A Memory' vibe, so we slowed it down a little and put a bit of our own spin on it.

4. You also toured with Michael Monroe. How was that experience? We've heard he is one of the nicest men in rock music.

HCSS: He was great, the whole tour was a blast and we thought we were the biggest Alice Cooper fans but we were wrong… it's definitely Michael! We spent many nights on the bus listening and talking about music, his music knowledge and appreciation is phenomenal.

5. Can you tell us about the upcoming album? What kind of sound/vibe does it have? Are there any songs that you are really excited to have your fans hear?

HCSS: The album has been written with our fans and live shows very much in mind, we're excited for the fans to hear every song but we're really excited to play the title track live as we feel it is an uplifting anthem for everything we believe in.

6. We were front row for that 2015 sold-out show at the Whisky A Go-Go in Hollywood, CA. Your performance of "Someone Special" still blows my mind. Do you remember that show? You guys totally killed it, one of the best shows I've ever seen live.

HCSS: Thank you, we loved it. The whole vibe of being on the strip and playing a sold out show was something we'll never forget. Can't wait to do it again.

7. Do you enjoy touring in the US? How does it differ from touring other countries…and any plans to tour the new album over here?

HCSS: We spend longer on the bus travelling as the shows are further apart but we loved playing in the States. At the moment we have one show booked for 2019 in Atlanta but we're hopefully going to be booking more once the album is out.

8. For a decade we've been saying that if you guys would have started in 1985, you'd be ranked right beside Guns N Roses, Van Halen and Metallica. What bands did you guys admire….and if you could tour the new album with any band in the world, who would you choose?

HCSS: Thank you so much, you just named three bands that we absolutely love, a tour with any of those would be fantastic. We've been lucky enough to do shows with some of our idols like Motorhead, KISS and AC/DC over the years. We're open to offers but a tour with someone like Maiden, Volbeat or GnR would be awesome

9. I've been to a hundred rock concerts and can honestly say that without a doubt, you guys are one of the top 4-5 live performers I've ever seen. How come you guys haven't released a live album?

HCSS: Hmm good question, We've thought about it and we've released live b' sides (as well as the video for 'Last Call For Alcohol') I'm sure we'll do one when we feel the time is right.

10. You guys are an amazing live band. Do you take pride in your life performances?

HCSS: Yes 100%, what's the point in being a band if you can't do it live?

11. The band's sound always changes from album to album, kind of like old school Motley Crue. You've got your Punk album, a hard rock one, more commercial rock sound, more metal sound....every album sounds different than the prior one. Is that a conscious effort on your part? Or is it just how it works out.

HCSS: A bands recording career is like a story that flows with ups and downs, fast action parts and slower more thoughtful parts. We never really wanted to make the same album twice, its about growth and moving forward. We write songs that reflect how we feel at the time.

12. How does Joakim Berg keep his voice so strong? So many rock singers in their 40s have lost most of their power and range. But he still sounds as awesome as you did a decade ago. How does he do it?

HCSS: Alcohol, and lots of it!! … All joking aside, he's very disciplined and takes care of himself. He puts a lot of work into what he does, as we all do.

13. In our book, we've ranked who we feel are the top current sleaze metal bands still performing today. It's based on bands whose careers (basically) have been during the 2000s. It's based on albums and how good the band is live. We've got Hardcore Superstar listed as the best band alive!!! Thoughts on that?

HCSS: We're blown away, thank you!! As you know, we pride ourselves on our live shows and there are so many great live bands out there that it's an honor just to be considered, cheers!!

13. Rounding out the top 10 are these bands – any thoughts on any of them? Shameless, Reckless love, The Last Vegas, Crashdiet, Santa Cruz, Crazy Lixx, Hell in the Club, Babylon Bombs. Do you guys know or like any of them?

HCSS: There's a few of them that we know quite well and we've played with a number of them over the years. They're all great bands

14. We've also ranked the top hair metal / sleaze rock songs/albums of All Time. We've done a year-by-by breakdown. Can you share your thoughts on these songs and albums? If they mean anything special, or any cool stories about recording them, etc:

15. In 2007…we've ranked "Dreamin' in a Casket" as the number one song of the year.

HCSS: We started to work on what would become "Dreamin' in a Casket" early 2007. We really felt inspired and knew we had something special early in the making because all these ideas just came flying. We've never done an album that hard before which meant that we had so many ideas to put into songs. It was a whole new world for us to write songs combining thrash and sleaze. We've always felt that both sleaze and thrash had so much in common and there were almost no bands before us to blend those styles into one. Both styles came from punk rock and hard rock. We recorded the drums at In Flames studio and finished it in my barn outside my house. A very fun and easy album to make.

16. In 2005… we've ranked We Don't Celebrate Sundays as the best song of the year.

HCSS: "The black album" was written over a period of two years when the band was not doing a whole lot. I've just moved out to the countryside and suddenly had lots of space to go bananas. Martin and I worked hard and wrote many songs. I did not communicate so much with the other members at this time. We needed a break from each other. When Martin and I felt that we were sitting on an amazing album we slowly contacted the others and we had a meeting. We all agreed to make just one more album together. It was a hard album to make because there were only a few people who believed in us at this time. No one really believed in that album except for the band members and our manager. We decided to start our own record label and release it there. The rest is history as they say.

17. In 2003 … we've ranked No Regrets as the number one album of the year, and Still I'm Glad as the number one song of the year.

HCSS: *No Regrets* was really hard to make. The band had toured constantly for three years and we never stopped partying. Writing the songs was pretty easy. The hard part was to get the band into the studio. I think the songs are great but the production is horrible to be honest. It was time for a break.

18. In 2015…..we ranked HCSS as the number one album of the year. And Touch The Sky as the second best song of the year.

HCSS: HCSS is a special album. Compared to all the other albums. It's more dark and serious. Both the songs and the lyrics. It was the album we needed to make at that specific moment.

The really cool thing about the album is that we got a chance to fly over to LA and sit down with Joe Barresi and see a master at work. Special experience indeed.

Touch The Sky - I remember us taking the writing of that song on the road - The song got finished in the back of the tour bus in the middle of nowhere.

19. In 2013 …we've got Long Time No See as the best ballad of the year.

HCSS: A cool and emotional ballad that was a perfect album finisher. It was a pleasure playing it live.

20. You guys are the only band that has five songs ranked as the top song of the year (that includes GnR, Bon Jovi, Def Leppard, Motley Crue, etc).

HCSS: Wow that's awesome!!

21. What bands do you admire?

HCSS: There's so many, KISS, AC/DC, Pantera, Motley, Death Angel, GnR, King Diamond... we could do this for hours

22. Is there any message you want to share with your fans?

HCSS: Thank you for all the support, we love you and we're looking forward to getting back to the States for more shows in 2019, and remember... You Can't Kill My Rock 'n Roll!!

LOVE RAZER

Photo courtesy of the official Love Razer webpage, photo by Jenna Middleton.

1. How big is the hair metal / hard rock scene in Canada right now?

LOVE RAZER: There isn't much of a scene where we are (Windsor, On). There is a little more of scene in Toronto but it still isn't anything overwhelming by any means. It defiantly seems bigger in the US and especially Europe.

2. When is your full length album coming out?

LOVE RAZER: Our full length album *Border City Rebels* came out April 23 2018. The album release show was April 28th in Windsor at Rockstar Music Hall

3. Do you plan on touring the states when it does?

LOVE RAZER: We would like to hit the States as soon as we can, once we can swing it we will be there \m/.

4. Who was the band's biggest influences?

LOVE RAZER: As individuals are tastes/influences defiantly vary, but as a band we can defiantly agree on Guns 'n' Roses & Motley Crue.

5. How would you describe your sound? For somebody curious about your band, what bands would you say you sound like?

LOVE RAZER: High octane rock n roll, big riffs, big choruses with a shit ton of attitude. We have been compared to sounding like a modern GNR or Motley Crue. But we try to have our own style and sound that defines us from everyone else.

6. Got any crazy touring/recording stories you can share?

LOVE RAZER: There are always crazy stories! We have had lots of stuff happen to us like women jumping on stage and flashing the audience, women throwing their panties at us, Sydney Snow has blown the crotch out of a couple pair of pants trying to imitate David Lee Roth. We had a drunk heckler at one show who we called on stage and the entire audience booed him out of the venue. We then saw a female choking him out in the parking lot. We have made ourselves throw up because we knew we shouldn't have ate that egg roll..but we were really hungry at the time...even if the meat was pink. Among many other crazy rock n roll adventures and many more to come!

7. In our opinion, Slik Toxik was the premier Canadian hair metal band. Are you guy's fans?

LOVE RAZER: A couple of us really dig them!

8. What bands would you guys most like to tour with if you could choose anybody!

LOVE RAZER: Guns 'n' Roses, Slash & Myles Kennedy and The Conspirators.

9. Can you give us a brief history of how you guys started out, who is in the band, how long together, etc.

LOVE RAZER: Metal Mike & Micky Bonez were in a tribute band together (found each other through Kijiji) then met Crissy Stixx. When they met Crissy they were already working on originals and recording them at Metal Mikes. After jamming the originals live for the first time at Bonez they knew they were onto something special. After trying out numerous singers the final day before our "looking for a singer" ad expired Sydney Snow sent us a message. We kind of laughed it off and were just about ready to give up on finding the right singer he then burst through the door and we started to jam "Home Sweet Home" and since that moment, Löve Razër was born...we are the 4 original members and it wouldn't be the same with anybody else. We have been a band for just over 2 years now

10. Any cool or funny (or bad) stories about playing with Gilby, Marq Torien, LA Guns or then Enuff Z'Nuff boys? Were they all cool, nice to you, any of them dicks, etc

LOVE RAZER: They were all really cool dudes, no crazy stories as they are pretty laid back guys it seems now. Chip was pretty funny though, he was always cracking jokes and at the beginning of our show Sydney ran out on stage with a high scream saying "what's up motherfuckers!?!" Then when Enuff Z'Nuff started. Chip came out and imitated Sydney by doing the high voice to!! Then after the first song he said "shout out to the real musicians keeping rock n roll alive" while pointing at us. So that was a pretty cool moment for us. What was also kind of weird, for the Gilby show we actually closed out the night. So it was pretty surreal to watch Gilby Clark on stage saying "who's ready for Löve Razër?!"

https://www.facebook.com/loverazerband
https://loverazer.com

Max Perenchio
Bad City

Photo courtesy of Mr. Perenchio's official Facebook page.

1. We have Welcome to the Wasteland as the 35th best album for the 2000-2017 era. And the 158 best overall album in the 1981-2017. Are you proud of that album and time of your career?

Perenchio: Totally, it's an absolute gonzo rock album; I really enjoyed writing and recording it. I listened to it the other day for the first time in a while, and it still knocks!

2. You guys had a pretty heavyweight backing core. Johnny K producing, toured with big names, big stars singing your praises. How come Atlantic didn't push for a second album?

Perenchio: Praises don't necessarily lead to album sales. It was tremendously out of place from a marketing perspective; also the band just gradually dissolved.

3. You toured with the Smashing Pumpkins in 2010. How was that? How did they treat you? Billy Corgan rumored to be a big-ego guy, how was it working with him?

Perenchio: Billy was a hero growing up and has always been awesome to me. He's a funny dude with a lot of knowledge and perspective, also one of the most underrated guitarists ever. Jeff is one of my closest friends here in Chicago, one of the most hilarious guys you'll ever meet. Great people in Pumpkinland!

4. Paul Stanley said "an absolute knockout and the best album I've heard in ages." How did it feel to get that kind of endorsement from a legendary figure like him? Were you guys Kiss fans growing up?

Perenchio: I almost flipped over my table when I read that quote. We were giant KISS fans. Actually at the time I was especially into the non-makeup years: "Animalize", "Lick It Up", "Asylum" etc. Touring with them was unforgettable.

5. You guys also toured with Slash and Hinder. Did you get to spend much time with Slash? How was that, how did he treat you guys?
Were you able to learn anything from him guitar-wise? Was he somebody you admired in your early days as a guitar player?

Perenchio: Hinder was insane. Those guys partied so hard and I saw some truly unique things on that tour bus. They were probably the youngest band we toured with and they raged with a level of intensity that I haven't seen since. Great guys.

Slash is a legend plain and simple. A rock icon, but unbelievably chill. Incredibly humble and down to earth, I honestly couldn't believe how kind he was on a day-to-day basis. He gave us notes on our set, he told us stories, he was unreal. You learn something from everyone but the secrets I learned from Slash I ain't telling anyone.

6. What would you be more interested in hearing this year - a new GnR album with Slash/Duff rejoining Axl. Or an ACDC album with Axl on vocals?

Perenchio: Definitely ACDC because it's a weirder situation that hasn't been recorded before. I would be excited to hear what Angus and Axl come up with; such a bizarre combination of rock energy. The existing GnR catalog is short and spotless, not sure I really need to hear a new one.

7. What were you doing before Bad City? Playing in bands, etc?

Perenchio: Yep, always had a band since I was like 12.

8. Alec Cyganowski filled in, who is a great singer. How come you guys then decided to disband the group? You had the backing of some heavyweights of the music industry, a great debut album, you guys had the look, the sound…..why did you guys call it quits?

Perenchio: By the end the band was just burnt out, 2/5 original members were gone, living in a practice space in Burbank California, drinking all day, writing a bloated rock opera that was too ambitious to ever finish, it was time to hang it up.

9. You had a great quote about the definition of Hair Metal and you guys being jammed into that classification. We've ran into the same problem and have used the term just because it neatly wraps up a sound/era. We've broken it in two – bands like Poison and Bon Jovi fit into the "hair band" category and then heavier bands like Guns N' Roses and Skid Row would be the "hair metal" side of things. But like you said, it is really just a title. We've tried to come up with another name, that people would hear and instantly know what type of music we were talking about. Arena Rock. Sleaze metal. PLEASE help us and solve the mystery!!! Give us a better name….and we'll name our book after it too! Save us!!!!

Perenchio: I think "hair metal" works for conveying what I think you're talking about, that 80s Sunset Strip sound. I really hate what "METAL" has become, like guttural Viking chants with zero dynamics; to me, metal still means Judas Priest. With that in mind, White Lion and Poison have some very metal moments! For Bad City there was a giant Arena Rock influence like Def Lep/Boston/Queen as well, but yeah I think labels are just for describing something quickly, there's not a lot of substance behind them.

10. How would you describe the sound of The Gold Web?

Perenchio: It's a big wild Glam band with modern and vintage elements. There's Bowie, Beatles, Flaming Lips, and a lot of modern psych inclinations, but also tons of harmonized guitar solos on the new record! The show is insane; tons of glitter, balloons, confetti, drag queens, total madness.

11. You guys dress in the crazy costumes and outfits. What inspired that?

Perenchio: KISS!!!

12. You just released a new album - _Acidchrist Superspice & the Candyboys_ – how has the reaction been? Can you tell us a little about the album? The vision, how long it took to write, who were the main writers, etc.

Perenchio: I love it, we're actually on tour as I'm talking to you. The album is kind of a beautiful mess, lots of magical glam sparkles and absurd psychedelic qualities mixed with very classic rock and roll. Listen to "Stargirl" if you're in a rush and want to get an idea. It's sort of a concept album, it took a few months to write, I generally write the songs, but the group sometimes helps me jam them out.

13. Do you pride yourself more on your song writing abilities or as your guitar musicianship?

Perenchio: Hmmm, good question, I value both of them these days but I'd have to say guitar solos aren't very cool if there's no song.

14. Jake Serek stayed with you. How's he as a bass player, band member and friend?

Perenchio: Best bass player around! Great dude too, check out his bass company SEREK BASSES.

15. What guitar players were your inspiration as a young musician?

Perenchio: When I was a kid I'd say Hendrix, Corgan, and Gilmour were pretty dominant. As I got a lil older Brian May, Frehley, Iommi, Van Halen.

16. If you could take _The Gold Web_ out on tour to support the new album and you could pick any band in the world to tour with – who would it be?

Perenchio: If only Bowie was alive... Out of a living band I think we would fit really well opening up for The Flaming Lips.

17. What advice would you give to a young guitar player who has dreams of making it as a professional guitar player? What techniques should he practice? What common mistakes to avoid? Is it better to get an instructor or to learn on your own (like pick a song you love and learn how to play it)?

Perenchio: I taught myself so I'm partial to that, but I've also taught hundreds and hundreds of students over the years so I see the value in both. All art is about finding yourself through stealing from others. Be bold, try to stand out, I love tasteless overblown gonzo nonsense more than I love gentle indie twee. Don't be afraid to be ridiculous.

18. You guys toured with Kiss. The question everybody probably asks you…..does Paul wear a wig?

Perenchio: Hahaha. I would be stripped of all my secret KISS credentials if I gave that one away.

19. Are you related to Hollywood dealmaker Jerry Perenchio? He died a couple months ago and is selling his Bel-Air mansion for a cool 350 million dollars.

Perenchio: Holy shit I wish I was. To my knowledge there are two "unrelated" clans of Perenchios that both come from nearby villages in Italy. My best guess is that they were related a very very long time ago and some Cain and Abel shit went down.

20. We read a quote where you said you were just chatting with Richie Sambora. How does that happen??? Were you just randomly chilling at his house?

Perenchio: Just at a club in New York after a Pumpkins show. He was nice.

21. What do you think about the career of a band like Bon Jovi. Started off as a hard rock band, then went to the hair band stage, then went to a more mature adult rock phase, and now seems to be going down the country-rock-soccer-mom era.

Perenchio: I mean I've gone through enough phases myself that I get it, you have to keep it fresh. I say hell yeah to anything that keeps the train going, I don't know a lot of Bon Jovi deep cuts, nor did I ever get way into them outside their big hits but I think it's dope that his real name is John Bongiovi.

22. Quick reaction (one word or one sentence) response when you see these names:

Paul Stanley: The Voice of Satan
Gene Simmons: Alpha male
Hinder: Jagermeister sponsorship
Slash: Human pinball machine
Smashing Pumpkins: Goth Mermaids
Jack White: "I'm goin' to Wichita!"
Ed Van Halen: Beethoven on heroin
Jimi Hendrix: 420
Richie Sambora: Cowboy hats

https://www.facebook.com/max.perenchio.9

Dito Godwin
Multi-platinum award winning producer
Motley Crue, Great White, No Doubt, Peter Criss

Picture of Mr. Godwin courtesy of his official Twitter page.

1. You were part of Reel to Reel productions in the late 80s focusing on Sunset Strip bands. What was that like? Was the Strip as crazy as us fans have been led to believe? Can you share some crazy stories with us!!!

Godwin:
First (Real to Reel Productions). The scene on the Sunset Strip in the 80s was wilder and crazier then you can believe. I wouldn't believe it but I was there and part of it. The Whisky, The Roxy, Gazzarri's and the Central (the viper room) were the hot spots on Sunset.

The Sunset Strip was so crowded it was hard to walk from 9pm till 2am. Packed every weekend!!!!!!! Guys with big hair, spandex, the biggest of dreams and young beautiful girls dressed like you can imagine everywhere. I don't wish to share any crazy stories LOL. it was a great time, I was in the studio producing 4 to 5 times a week every week, big label projects and brand new bands just arriving in LA.

2. What bands did you work with?

Godwin:
Too many to name. From all over the world coming to Hollywood to make it happen. My reputation with bands in LA was strong, so I got a ton of fucking work.

3. From those years you must have witnessed hundreds of bands. Who were the most amazing ones to see live (back then, in their early days). And were there bands that you were surprised didn't make it……or that you still can't believe they DID make it big?

Godwin:
All of the above "YES" I produced No Doubt's first Interscope CD and it was no shock when they made it. I promoted Motley Crue *Too Fast for Love* in 1981, no surprise they made it.

4. Then you founded TnT records in 1991. Most successful bands/albums that you worked with?

Godwin:
I signed Peter Criss of KISS and recorded two CDs with him, one of which featured KISS legend Ace Frehley.

5. You've also taught Music business management and studio productions at several universities, including UCLA. Teaching college aged kids is a bit different than working with Motley Crue! How and why did you get into that line of work?

Godwin:
I had bad teachers my entire life so I decided to be a great teacher. I have been teaching
Music Business Management and Studio Production including, UCLA, SOU, University of Sound Arts and MI to mention a few. I've taught for over 25 years and love it.

6. You play multiple instruments, which do you enjoy the most and what are you the best at? Did you ever want to be a professional musician?

Godwin:
I have spent the most time playing guitar and bass. In my heart I'm a drummer because that's how I started in rock. Thank you Beatles. My friend and I walked home after seeing HELP The Beatles. On the way home I turned to him and said "now I know what I want to do." He agreed. We still make music together to this day professionally.

7. If a billionaire gave you a blank check and you could spend it producing/working with any 2-3 bands next year….who would you choose, or what bands would you choose to work with?

Godwin:

First Justin Bieber, Beck and Soilwork.

8. Would you be willing to tackle an Axl Rose/Guns N Roses album?

Godwin:
Bring it on!!!!! And they would love it!! Including Axl! No Doubt!

9. What was your involvement or connection with Black Sabbath? Your Wiki page says you toured with the band.

Godwin:
In the early 70s I played several festivals as an opening act for Black Sabbath. A great memory.

10. You founded EFM records in 2008. Is that your main gig today? What bands are you most proud of?

Godwin:
EFM records was a short-lived project distributed by Universal. It was great experience and I worked with some very talented artist. Including the late great Kevin Carlberg!!!

11. Can you share some thoughts on a few of the amazing bands you've worked with The good/bad/ugly/etc!

Godwin:
Great working with No Doubt. Great working with The KISS guys. Great working with the Great White guys. Incredible working with Jani Lane. There are so few bad or ugly projects that I have done that they are not worth mentioning.
Before I work with a client, we have established a relationship and we go into the studio focused and confident.

12. Jani Lane, Jaberwocky. Jani is our second favorite rock singer of all time. We love that you worked/recorded with him. Would love to hear any stories you want to share.

Godwin:
In the mid to late 90s I was working with Jani at a killer studio in North Hollywood "Jandermonium". We recorded four songs in three days. The last day I turned to Jani and said "we only have four hours of studio time left (on his way to Washington for a tour) and you haven't sung one song."

Jani said "Don't worry man I've got this" and in three hours sang his ass off on all four tunes including backing vocals. The tracks came out incredible!!! I was so impressed with Jani. At the end of the night Jani turned to me and said "Dito you blew my mind" That made me feel great.

We later worked together in 2011 our plan was to write for Jani and then sign him to my Universal deal and write for other artists as well. He appeared on That Metal Show and talked about working with me during the summer instead of touring. A bunch of my friends called me and said "Holy shit I heard Jani talking about you last night!"
How cool is that?!!!

13. You also helped break No Doubt, how was the experience working with that band?

Godwin:
I loved working with No Doubt, they were great even back then. Gwen was the most prepared artist I had ever worked with. Tracks from this self-titled CD have found their way onto five other No Doubt CDs through out the years. Producing this bands first cd changed both of our lives for the better.

MUTT and DESMOND

We all know who Bon Jovi and Def Leppard are. We know what they look like, sound like, we know the band's history. We know their popular albums from front-to-back and the songs word-for-word.

But if you aren't a total die-hard fan of the bands there are two names you might not be familiar with. And without these two guys, two hair metal legends might not have grown beyond being opening acts or small arena level bands.

Desmond Child
From Livin' La Vida Loca to I Hate Myself For Loving You

Whatever your favorite Bon Jovi song is, Child most likely had a hand in writing it. He collaborated with the band on 28 different tunes, including their biggest and most legendary hits.

You Give Love a Bad Name – check.
Livin' on a Prayer – check.
Bad Medicine – check.
Keep the Faith – check.
Born to be My Baby – check.
Hearts Breaking Even – check.
And the list continues to include 22 other classic songs.

Child was more than just a scribe for the New Jersey rockers. He is also a master songwriter for many different artists in several different genres. In the rock world, he has written hits for Aerosmith (Dude Looks Like a Lady, Crazy and What it Takes), Poison by Alice Cooper, Lovin' You's a Dirty Job and Givin' Yourself Away by Ratt and several songs for Kiss, including I Was Made for Loving You, Heaven's on Fire and Let's Put the X in Sex.

Child also wrote songs for Vince Neil and Sebastian Bach.

Outside of the genre, Child wrote hit songs for artists like Ricky Martin, Cher, Joan Jett, Dream Theatre, Selena Gomez and Kelly Clarkson. He is in the Songwriters Hall of Fame, earning that honor after writing more than 70 songs that have charted on the Billboard top 40. His songs have appeared on albums that have sold more than 300 million copies.

Child got his first big break in 1979 when he co-wrote the song I Was Made for Loving You for Kiss on their Dynasty album. To this day, it still ranks as one of the band's most successful songs.

Paul Stanley passed Child's number and information on to fellow musicians Jon Bon Jovi and Richie Sambora. Child reportedly joined JBJ and Sambora in the basement of Richie's parent's house. The three quickly penned You Give Love a Bad Name which would go on to become Bon Jovi's first number one hit. Two more number one smashes soon followed – Livin' on a Prayer and Bad Medicine – and the rest is history.

"The Desmond you don't know about," says Jon Bon Jovi, "is the one who not only taught me the next level of songwriting, but so many of the true aspects of friendship: truth, honor and loyalty. We've been through a lot together – the ups and the downs…and the ups again." (Desmond Child Wikipedia Page).

With Child's help, Bon Jovi is considered one of the Mt. Rushmore artists of the hair metal genre. Without his help they possibly fall down to the LA Guns and Winger level.

The Success of Def Leppard

While Bon Jovi was still able to write, record and release several billboard hits and albums on their own merits, Mutt Lange has been the engine behind the Def Leppard train of success.

Lange's career has been off the charts. Unparalleled in the industry, Lange might be the most successful writer/producer in music history.

Def Leppard released two of the most iconic rock albums in music history: *Pyromania* in 1983, followed up by *Hysteria* in 1987.

Pyromania was one of the albums that really kicked off the hair metal era and its 10-million plus in sales has landed it as many rock fans favorite DL album. Lange co-wrote every song on the album, including classics like Photograph and Rock of Ages.

Lange secured his role as the ultimate hair metal songwriter on Leppard's follow-up album *Hysteria*. Lange was scheduled to produce *Hysteria* but had to drop out do to physical exhaustion. DL brought another producer on but the band couldn't ever get on the same page with the new guy. So Lange came back to save the day. And did he ever. Lange co-wrote every song on *Hysteria*, which went on to sell more than 25 million copies. Key songs include Pour Some Sugar on Me and the hit ballads Love Bites and the title track Hysteria.

Lange also produced two more Def Leppard albums. The critically acclaimed *High' N' Dry* (1981) and *Adrenalize* (also co-wrote most songs) in 1992, which sold several million copies and went to number one on the Billboard album charts. Lange co-wrote a couple songs for the 1999 album *Euphoria*, including the song Promises which went to #1 on the rock charts.

History

Lange received his big break while working with AC/DC. In 1979 the band wasn't happy with their current producer so they brought Lange in to see what he could do. Not only did he produce an album generally considered a rock masterpiece, but Lange also helped singer Bon Scott improve his studio vocals. And, just for fun, Lange also sang backup on several songs. *Highway to*

Hell went on to sell approximately 10 million copies and was the band's breakthrough album.

Unfortunately, Scott ended up passing away after the album's release. AC/DC decided to carry on, hiring new singer Brian Johnson and bringing Lange back into the studio for the follow-up to *Highway to Hell*.

Lange and the Young brothers turned their game up to even a higher level. Lange worked his studio magic with Johnson's vocals and pushed the rest of the band to create the best album they were capable of writing and recording. The result? *Back in Black*, released in 1980, which went on to sell more than 50 million copies and is the 2nd highest selling album of all time.

Lange produced one more album for the Australian rockers, their 1981 release – *For Those About to Rock* – which went on to occupy the number one album spot on Billboard. In spite of the overwhelming success that Lange brought to the band, AC/DC chose to go with other producers for the rest of their career, wanting to get back to the more "raw" sound the band had before Lange helped turned them into a more polished sounding hard rock band. AC/DC have released eight albums since moving on from Lange. Those eight albums combined sales are less than *Back in Black's* number of albums sold.

Lange's work with Def Leppard and AC/DC is enough to earn him a spot in the Rock and Roll Hall of Fame – as a writer and producer. But Lange proved he wasn't just a hard rock savant.

Lange's third member of his mighty trilogy is country singer Shania Twain. He produced and co-wrote her 1997 album *Come On Over*, which turned into the top selling country music album of all time, top selling studio album by a female with 40 million copies, the top selling album of the 1990s and the 9th best selling album in US history.

Lange also produced and co-wrote Twain's 1995 album *The Woman In Me* that sold more than 20 million copies. And 2002's *Up* which sold more than 15 million copies.

Not only did Lange work on one of the best hair metal albums of all time, one of the best rock albums of all time, and one of the best country albums of all time, but he also wrote and produced songs/albums for such artists as:
- Bryan Adams (co-wrote I Do It For You – which spent 16 weeks at #1 on the UK Billboard chart)
- Foreigner – 4
- The Cars – Heartbeat City
- Billy Ocean
- Michael Bolton
- Nickelback
- Maroon 5 – Hands All Over
- Muse - Drones
- Dionne Warwick
- Tina Turner – What's Love Got to Do With It
- Celine Dion
- Backstreet Boys – Backstreet's Back and Millennium
- Britney Spears – Oops!...I Did It Again
- Lady Gaga – Born This Way

Some of the most popular songs Lange wrote or co-work include:
*All For Love – Rod Stewart/Sting/Bryan Adams
*It's Gotta Be You – Backstreet Boys
*Said I Loved You But I Lied – Michael Bolton
*All I Wanna do Is Make Love To You – Heart
*Do You Believe in Love – Huey Lewis and the News
*Lovin' Every Minute of It – Loverboy
*Who Are You – Carrie Underwood
*Get Out of My Dreams, Get Into My Car – Billy Ocean

Lange has five Grammy Awards on his resume.

The Best of 2000-2017
Top Rock Songs
1. Caught in a Dream – Tesla (Into the Now, 2004)
2. Summer Song – Joey C. Jones (Melodies for the Masses, 2006)
3. Better – Guns N' Roses (Chinese Democracy, 2008)
4. Another Bad Day – Vince Neil (Tattoos & Tequila, 2010)
5. It's Not Enough – Tom Keifer (The Way Life Goes, 2013)
6. It's My Life – Bon Jovi (Crush, 2000)
7. Best of Me – Ratt (Infestation, 2010)
8. Face – Warrant (Under the Influence, 2001)
9. Don't You Cry – L.A. Guns (Waking the Dead, 2002)
10. I'm With You – Bon Jovi (What About Now, 2013)
11. Lay Down Your Love – Whitesnake (Good to be Bad, 2008)
12. Forever More – Tesla (Forever More, 2008)
13. Bag of Bones – Europe (Bag of Bones, 2012)
14. I Don't Mind – Great White (Rising, 2009)
15. Stained Glass Heart – Michael Monroe (Horns and Halos, 2013)
16. So Divine – Tesla (Simplicity, 2014)
17. TWAT – Guns N' Roses (Chinese Democracy, 2008)
18. Moonshine – Hardcore Superstar (Split Your Lip, 2010)
19. As Good as it Gets – Ratt (Infestation, 2010)
20. Everyday – Bon Jovi (Bounce, 2002)
21. Between You and Me – D-A-D (Soft Dogs, 2002)
22. We Don't Celebrate Sundays – HCSS (Hardcore Superstar, 2005)
23. What Kind of Man – KINGOFTHEHILL (Unreleased, 2005)
24. If I Die Tomorrow – Motley Crue (Red, White & Crue, 2005)
25. Can You Hear the Wind Blow – Whitesnake (Good To Be Bad, 2008)
26. 2nd Street – Tesla (Twisted Wires & The Acoustic Sessions, 2011)
27. Save Her – Crashdiet (Generation Wild, 2010)
28. Still I'm Glad – Hardcore Superstar (No Regrets, 2003)
29. Still Kickin' – Danger Danger (Cockroach, 2001)

30. Lovin' a Girl Like You – Danger Danger (Rare Cuts, 2003)
31. The Devil Made Me Do It – L.A. Guns (The Missing Peace, 2017)
32. You're Gone – Kix (Rock Your Face Off, 2014)
33. We Don't Run – Bon Jovi (Burning Bridges, 2015)
34. Words Can't Explain – Tesla (Into the Now, 2004)
35. City of Angeles – L.A. Guns (Waking the Dead, 2002)
36. Something for You – Great White (Elated, 2012)
37. Touch the Sky - Hardcore Superstar (HCSS, 2015)
38. Dreamin' in a Casket – HCSS (Dreamin' in a Casket, 2007)
39. Gonna Get Ready – Europe (Last Look at Eden, 2009)
40. We are the Ones to Fall – Santa Cruz (Santa Cruz, 2015)
41. Better Off Without U – Shameless (Famous 4 Madness, 2007)
42. Liberation – HCSS (Bad Sneakers and a Pina Colada, 2000)
43. Please Me Tease Me – Shanghai (Take Another Bite, 2000)
44. Muse – Hell in the Club (Devil on My Shoulder, 2014)
45. Back to the Rhythm – Great White (Back to the Rhythm, 2007)
46. Honey Tongue – Hardcore Superstar (No Regrets, 2003)
47. Shades of Grey – Hardcore Superstar (Beg For It, 2009)
48. Babylon's Burning – Babylon Bombs (Babylon's Burning, 2009)
49. Love Me with Your Top Down – Kix (Rock Your Face Off, 2014)
50. Standing on the Outside – Dokken (Lightning Strikes Again, 2008)
51. Mine All Mine – Wig Wam (667 The Neighbour of the Beast, 2004)
52. Friends in Spirit – Kingdom Come (Ain't Crying for the Moon, 2006)
53. Outlaw – Crazy Lixx (Crazy Lixx, 2014)
54. Paper Heart – Vains of Jenna (The Art of Telling Lies, 2009)
55. Taste of It – Like an Army (Single 2013)
56. Love is a Bitchslap – Sebastian Bach (Angel Down, 2007)
57. Slave to Your Love – Wig Wam (Wig Wamania, 2006)
58. Don't Forget Me When I'm Gone – Alleycat Scratch (Last Call, 2010)
59. So What! – Tesla (Forever More, 2008)
60. Love Drug – Vain (All Those Strangers, 2010)
61. Shame – Hardcore Superstar (Thank You, 2001)
62. Beautiful – L.A. Guns (Man in the Moon, 2001)
63. Any Kinda Love – Jack Russell (For You, 2002)
64. All for Love – Whitesnake (Good to be Bad, 2008)
65. Queen 4 a Day – Shameless (Queen 4 a Day, 2000)

66. Lost in America – Mr. Big (Actual Size, 2001)
67. Hard to Get Over (You're So) – The Last Vegas (Eat Me, 2016)
68. Do You Want to Taste It – Wig Wam (Man in the Moon, 2010)
69. Evil Eyes – The Last Vegas (Bad Decisions, 2012)
70. Little Girl – Dokken (Long Way Home, 2002)
71. Heroes are Forever – Crazy Lixx (Loud Minority, 2007)
72. One More Minute – Hardcore Superstar (C'mon Take On Me, 2013)
73. Aiming High – Santa Cruz (Screaming for Adrenaline, 2013)
74. Stitches – Skid Row (United World Rebellion Chapter One, 2013)
75. Give Me a Reason – Dokken (Lighting Strikes Again, 2008)
76. Nervous Breakdown – Hardcore Superstar (Beg For It, 2009)
77. Last Look at Eden – Europe (Last Look at Eden, 2009)
78. See You Around – Skid Row (Thickskin, 2003)
79. Good Time – Danger, Danger (Paul Laine) (Cockroach, 2001)
80. Lazy Day – Enuff Z'Nuff (Dissonance, 2010)
81. Misunderstood – Bon Jovi (Bounce, 2002)
82. We are the Weekend – Reckless Love (Invader, 2016)
83. Young Blood Rising – Santa Cruz (Bad Blood Rising, 2017)
84. Undefeated – Def Leppard (Mirror Ball – Live & More, 2011)
85. Touch – Bad City (Welcome To The Wasteland, 2010)
86. Set it Off – Vains of Jenna (Lit Up/Let Down, 2006)
87. I'm Bad – The Last Vegas (Whatever Gets You Off, 2009)
88. Revolution – L.A. Guns (Waking the Dead, 2002)
89. I Wanna Live – Babylon A.D. (American Blitzkrieg, 2000)
90. Party Til' I'm Gone – Hardcore Superstar (HCSS, 2015)
91. Tonight – Motley Crue (Too Fast For Love Reissue, 2003)
92. Breakin' Free – Tesla (Forever More, 2008)
93. She Needs Me – TnT (My Religion, 2004)
94. Give Me a Sign – Ammunition (Shanghaied, 2015)
95. Love Don't Live Here – Jack Russell (He Saw it Comin', 2017)
96. Torn to Shreds – Def Leppard (X, 2002)
97. Cut From the Same Cloth – Junkyard (High Water, 2017)
98. Push & Pull – Keel (Streets of Rock & Roll, 2010)
99. Wild Boys – Hardcore Superstar (Hardcore Superstar, 2005)
100. Music Man – Warrant (Louder Harder Faster, 2017)
101. Allright – D-A-D (Scare Yourself, 2005)

102. Standing on the Verge – HCSS (Hardcore Superstar, 2005)
103. Night on Fire – Reckless Love (Spirit, 2013)
104. Who Says You Can't Go Home – Bon Jovi (Have a Nice Day, 2005)
105. Wait All Night – Joey C Jones (Melodies for the Masses, 2006)
106. Devil on My Shoulder – Hell in the Club (Devil on My Shoulder, 2014)
107. Hollywood Forever – L.A. Guns (Hollywood Forever, 2012)
108. Six Million Dollar Man – Danger, Danger (The Return of the Gildersleeves, 2000)
109. The Life & Death of Mr. Nobody – Hell in the Club (Shadow of the Monster, 2016)
110. Sea of Love – Def Leppard (Def Leppard, 2015)
111. Give it the Gun – Skid Row (United World Rebellion Chapter Two, 2014)
112. Blue Skies – Shark Island (Gathering of the Faithful, 2006)
113. Catcher in the Rye – Guns N' Roses (Chinese Democracy, 2008)
114. Down and Dirty – Deaf, Dumb & Blond (L.A. Days, 2017)
115. Temptation – Sebastian Bach (Give 'Em Hell, 2014)
116. Steal Your Heart Away – Whitesnake (Forevermore, 2011)
117. It's a Miracle – Crashdiet (Rest in Sleaze, 2005)
118. The Last Goodbye – Dokken (Hell to Pay, 2004)
119. The Distance – Bon Jovi (Bounce, 2002)
120. Lonely Road – Killer Dwarfs (Start @ One, 2013)
121. Buried Unkind – Steelheart (Good 2B Alive, 2008)
122. Have a Nice Day – Bon Jovi (Have a Nice Day, 2005)
123. Hollywood Ending – Motley Crue (Tattoo You, 2000)
124. Wimpy Sister – Hardcore Superstar (Thank You, 2001)
125. Deliver Me – Fastway (Eat Dog Eat, 2011)
126. Always the Pretender – Europe (Secret Society, 2006)
127. Everything I Own – Tesla (A Peace of Time, 2007)
128. Undertow – Mr. Big (What If..., 2011)
129. Love Blind – Babylon A.D. (Lost Sessions, 2014)
130. Keep it Up All Night – Reckless Love (Invader, 2016)
131. Don't Mean Shit – Hardcore Superstar (HCSS, 2015)
132. Save it for Yourself – KINGOFTHEHILL (Unreleased, 2005)
133. Rock Down This Place – Hell in the Club (Let the Games Begin, 2011)
134. Animal Attraction – Reckless Love (Animal Attraction, 2011)

135. Breaking All the Rules – Wig Wam (Wig Wamania, 2006)
136. Falling Rain – Crashdiet (The Unattractive Revolution, 2007)
137. Hello, Hello – TnT (Atlantis, 2008)
138. Bleed – Private Line (21st Century Pirates, 2004)
139. Fashion - Hanoi Rocks (Street Poetry, 2007)
140. Blue Eyed Soul – Sweet FA (The Lost Tapes, 2007)
141. Living a World Away – Tora Tora (Revolution Day, 2011)
142. Look @ Me – Tesla (Into the Now, 2004)
143. Kings of Demolition – Skid Row (United World Rebellion Chapter One, 2013)
144. Faded – Junkyard (single, 2015)
145. All Out of Luck – Whitesnake (Forevermore, 2011)
146. Sick Little Twisted Mind – Danger, Danger (Ted Poley) (Cockroach, 2001)
147. Miss You – The Last Vegas (Sweet Salvation, 2014)
148. Last Time in Neverland – D-A-D (Dic-Nil-Lan-Daft-Erd-Ark, 2011)
149. Thorn in My Side – Bon Jovi (The Circle, 2009)
150. My Own Worst Enemy – Sebastian Bach (Kicking & Screaming, 2011)

Top Ballads:
1. Apologize – The Last Vegas (Whatever Gets You Off, 2009)
2. Far Away – Shameless (Queen 4 a Day, 2000)
3. By Your Side – Sebastian Bach (Angel Down, 2007)
4. Long Time No See – Hardcore Superstar (C'mon Take On Me, 2013)
5. Don't You Ever Leave Me – Hardcore Superstar (Bad Sneakers and a Pina Colada, 2000)
6. Fallin' Apart – Tesla (Forever More, 2008)
7. Anything it Takes – The Last Vegas (Eat Me, 2016)
8. Shelter From the Rain – Tora Tora (Revolution Day, 2011)
9. Long, Long Way to Go – Def Leppard (X, 2002)
10. What Do You Got – Bon Jovi (Greatest Hits, 2010)
11. Summer Rain – Whitesnake (Good to be Bad, 2008)
12. Run to Your Mama – Hardcore Superstar (Split Your Lip, 2010)
13. She's Not Coming Home Tonight – Shameless (Splashed, 2002)
14. Have You Seen Her – Bang Tango (Pistol Whipped in the Bible Belt, 2011)
15. How Many More Times – Hannon Tramp (Hannon Tramp, 2014)

16. Love Has it's Reasons – Shanghai (Bombs Away, 2001)
17. Street of Dreams – Guns N' Roses (Chinese Democracy, 2008)
18. Inside Outside Inn – Kix (Rock Your Face off, 2014)
19. Slip Away – Babylon Bombs (Doin' You Nasty, 2006)
20. Here Comes that Sick Bitch Again – Hardcore Superstar (Split Your Lip, 2010)
21. Tried and True – Junkyard – (Tried and True, 2003)
22. My Sanctuary – Great White (Risen, 2009)
23. Selflove-Sick – Private Line (21st Century Pirates, 2004)
24. It's Alright – Babylon Bombs (Babylon's Burning, 2009)
25. Just Yesterday – Great White (Back to the Rhythm, 2007)
26. The Sky's Falling – Babylon A.D. (American Blitzkrieg, 2000)
27. Get Me Out of California – Santa Cruz (Bad Blood Rising, 2017)
28. This is Killing Me – Skid Row (United World Rebellion Chapter One, 2013)
29. We All Fall Down – D-A-D (Dic-Nil-Lan-Daft-Erd-Ark, 2011)
30. All I Want All I Need – Whitesnake (Good to be Bad, 2008)
31. I Don't Think I Love U – Shameless (Queen 4 a Day, 2000)
32. Nothing Like it in the World – Mr. Big (Actual Size, 2001)
33. Naked – Hell in the Club (Shadow of the Monster, 2016)
34. B-Song – Tora Tora (Miss B Haven, 2009)
35. Falling Into You – Sebastian Bach (Angel Down, 2007)
36. New Love in Town – Europe (Last Look at Eden, 2009)
37. You Showed Me – Tom Keifer (The Way Life Goes, 2013)
38. Tell Me Where to Go – Wig Wam (667 The Neighbour of the Beast, 2004)
39. Cross My Heart – Tesla (Simplicity, 2014)
40. Goodbye My Friend – Dokken (Long Way Home, 2002)
41. What of Our Love – Crazy Lixx (New Religion, 2010)
42. Whatever it Takes – Jack Russell (For You, 2002)
43. Take Me Home – White Lion (Return of the Pride, 2008)
44. Only You – Tesla (Into the Now, 2004)
45. I Live For You – Harry Hess (Living in Yesterday, 2012)
46. Anything for You – Jack Russell (He Saw it Comin', 2017)
47. Mother's Love – Hardcore Superstar (Thank You, 2001)
48. U in My Life – Warrant (Louder Harder Faster, 2017)
49. Madagascar – Guns N' Roses (Chinese Democracy, 2008)
50. Disposable – Mark Slaughter (Halfway There, 2017)
51. Man in the Moon – Wig Wam (Non Stop Rock 'N Roll, 2010)

52. One of These Days – Whitesnake (Forevermore, 2011)
53. Hot Rain – Reckless Love (Spirit, 2013)
54. Words Don't Count – White Lion (Lost Tracks, Demos and Oddities, 2009)
55. Love's Got Nothing on Me – The Last Vegas (Eat Me, 2016)
56. Scream – Tyketto (Reach, 2016)
57. Catch Your Fall – Skid Row (United World Rebellion Chapter Two, 2014)
58. Star – Hell in the Club (Let the Games Begin, 2011)
59. Better Off Without You – Tesla (Twisted Wires & The Acoustic Sessions, 2011)
60. Most Important Thing – Bang Tango (Ready To Go, 2004)
61. Shouldn't Cry – Vain (All Those Strangers, 2010)
62. Real Love – Bon Jovi (This House is Not For Sale, 2016)
63. Hard to Say Goodbye – Great White (Elated, 2012)
64. At the End of the Day – Wig Wam (Wig Wamania, 2006)
65. Me and Dad – TnT (Atlantis, 2008)
66. Dead and Gone – Fastway (Eat Dog Eat, 2011)
67. Where R U – Pretty Boy Floyd (The Vault 2, 2003)
68. Underneath the Sun – L.A. Guns (Hollywood Forever, 2012)
69. Too Late for Love – Stage Dolls (Get a Life, 2004)
70. Tonight – KINGOFTHEHILL (Unreleased, 2005)
71. You Filled My Head – D-A-D (Scare Yourself, 2005)
72. Rescue Me – Tora Tora (Revolution Day, 2011)
73. I Remember – Dokken (Lighting Strikes Again, 2008)
74. Other Than Me – Tesla (Simplicity, 2014)
75. You Want to Make a Memory – Bon Jovi (Lost Highway, 2007)
76. Who Am I To Blame – Tora Tora (Miss B Haven, 2009)
77. Sacred Place – Paul Shortino's The Cutt (Sacred Place, 2002)
78. Had Enough – Sebastian Bach (Give 'Em Hell, 2014)
79. Somehow – Every Mother's Nightmare (Smokin' Delta Voodoo, 2000)
80. Afraid of Love – Danger, Danger (Ted Poley) (Cockroach, 2001)
81. Operator – Shameless (Splashed, 2002)
82. Let Me In – Great White (Full Circle, 2017)
83. The Man Who Has Everything – Mr. Big (The Stories We Could Tell, 2014)
84. Fantasy – Reckless Love (Animal Attraction, 2011)
85. Perfectly – TnT (My Religion, 2004)
86. I Believe – Tigertailz (Bezerk 2.0, 2006)

87. The Missing Kind – TnT (Atlantis, 2008)
88. It Can't Be that Bad – Shameless FT: Frankie Muriel (The Filthy 7, 2017)
89. Home – Like an Army (single release, 2013)
90. Don't Hide Your Heart – Shanghai (Take Another Bite, 2000)
91. Picture Yourself – Joey C. Jones (Melodies for the Masses, 2006)
92. Good Night – The Last Vegas (Bad Decisions, 2012)
93. Tonite – Tora Tora (Bombs Away, 2009)
94. Never Let You Go – White Lion (Return Of The Pride, 2008)
95. Through These Eyes – Shanghai (Bombs Away, 2001)
96. Just in Case – Tesla (Forever More, 2008)
97. Home – Warrant (Rockaholic, 2011)
98. After All This Time – Winger (Karma, 2009)
99. I Don't Want to be Happy – Mr. Big (Actual Size, 2001)

Top Albums
1. Waking the Dead – L.A. Guns - 2002
2. Infestation – Ratt - 2010
3. Chinese Democracy – Guns N' Roses - 2008
4. Angel Down – Sebastian Bach – 2007
5. Eat Me – The Last Vegas – 2016
6. Forevermore – Whitesnake – 2011
7. Dic-Nil-Lan-Daft-Erd-Ark – D-A-D - 2011
8. Bounce – Bon Jovi – 2002
9. No Regrets – Hardcore Superstar – 2003
10. Twelve Shots on the Rocks – Hanoi Rocks- 2002
11. Hardcore Superstar – Hardcore Superstar - 2005
12. Soft Dogs – D-A-D – 2002
13. Unreleased – KINGOFTHEHILL – 2005
14. The Missing Peace – L.A. Guns - 2017
15. Actual Size – Mr. Big – 2001
16. Into the Now – Tesla – 2004
17. Crush – Bon Jovi – 2000
18. Tried and True – Junkyard – 2003
19. Forever More – Tesla – 2008
20. Rising – Great White – 2009
21. Melodies for the Masses – Joey C. Jones - 2006

22. Split Your Lip – Hardcore Superstar – 2010
23. Good to be Bad – Whitesnake – 2008
24. All Those Strangers – Vain – 2010
25. Rest in Sleaze – Crashdiet – 2005
26. Dreamin' in a Casket – Hardcore Superstar – 2007
27. Wig Wamania – Wig Wam – 2006
28. Street Poetry – Hanoi Rocks – 2007
29. Rockaholic – Warrant - 2011
30. Back to the Rhythm – Great White - 2007
31. Last Look at Eden – Europe – 2009
32. Revolution Day – Tora Tora - 2011
33. Welcome to the Wasteland – Bad City - 2010
34. Tattoos & Tequila – Vince Neil -2010
35. Eat Dog Eat – Fastway – 2011
36. The Way Life Goes – Tom Keifer - 2013
37. Famous 4 Madness – Shameless - 2007
38. Lighting Strikes Again – Dokken - 2008
39. For You – Jack Russell - 2002
40. Hollywood Forever – L.A. Guns – 2012
41. Enough Rope – Vain – 2011
42. Twisted Wires & The Acoustic Sessions – Tesla - 2011
43. United World Rebellion Chapter One – Skid Row - 2013
44. Long Way Home – Dokken - 2002
45. Rolling with the Punches – Vain – 2017
46. Have a Nice Day – Bon Jovi – 2005
47. Let the Games Begin – Hell in the Club - 2011
48. Kicking & Screaming – Sebastian Bach - 2011
49. Dissonance – Enuff Z'Nuff – 2010
50. He Saw it Comin' – Jack Russell - 2017
51. Scare Yourself – D-A-D – 2005
52. Off Your Rocker – Jetboy – 2010
53. American Blitzkrieg – Babylon A.D. - 2000
54. Cockroach – Danger, Danger (Ted Poley), 2001
55. Pistol Whipped in the Bible Belt – Bang Tango - 2011
56. Bad Sneakers and a Pina Colada – Hardcore Superstar - 2000
57. 667 The Neighbour of the Beast – Wig Wam - 2004

58. X – Def Leppard – 2002
59. Animal Attraction – Reckless Love - 2011
60. New Religion – Crazy Lixx – 2010
61. Queen 4 a Day – Shameless – 2000
62. Babylon's Burning – Babylon Bombs – 2009
63. The Return of the Great Gildersleeves – Danger, Danger - 2000
64. Streets of Rock & Roll – Keel – 2010
65. Whatever Gets You Off – The Last Vegas - 2009
66. Start from the Dark – Europe – 2004
67. Generation Wild – Crashdiet – 2010
68. Smokin' Delta Voodoo – Every Mother's Nightmare - 2000
69. Rock Your Face Off – Kix - 2014
70. Take Another Bite – Shanghai – 2000
71. C'mon Take On Me – Hardcore Superstar - 2013
72. Man in the Moon – L.A. Guns – 2001
73. My Religion – TnT – 2004
74. HCSS – Hardcore Superstar - 2015
75. Santa Cruz – Santa Cruz - 2015
76. Blood Brothers – Rose Tattoo - 2007
77. Atlantis – TnT – 2008
78. Defying Gravity – Mr. Big - 2017
79. Screaming for Adrenaline – Santa Cruz - 2013
80. Shanghaied – Ammunition – 2015
81. Spirit – Reckless Love - 2013
82. Elation – Great White – 2012
83. Revelation Highway – Babylon A.D. - 2017
84. Splashed – Shameless – 2002
85. Simplicity – Tesla – 2014
86. …The Stories We Could Tell – Mr. Big - 2014
87. IV – Winger – 2006
88. Good 2B Alive – Steelheart - 2008
89. Non Stop Rock'n Roll – Wig Wam - 2010
90. Dial S for Sex – Shameless – 2011
91. Hannon Tramp – Hannon Tramp - 2014
92. Bad Decisions – The Last Vegas – 2012
93. Burning Bridges – Bon Jovi – 2015

94. Shadow of the Monster – Hell in the Club - 2016
95. New Tattoo – Motley Crue – 2000
96. Beg For It – Hardcore Superstar – 2009
97. Living in Yesterday – Harry Hess - 2012
98. Karma – Winger – 2009
99. Better Days Comin' – Winger - 2014
100. Return of the Pride – White Lion – 2008

THE FANS

This is just a fun little section where we honor some of the super fans out there. We've included die-hard fans thoughts on their favorite bands, band tattoos they've decorated their body with, and pictures they've taken with our favorite stars!

Bon Jovi Fan: Jaki@jakijellz (Twitter)

Bon Jovi just makes everything feel better. On a bad day, Jon's voice turns it around. They're there when everything else isn't.

Guns N' Roses Fan: BlueJeanBaby728 (Twitter)

I was in my 20's, had just had a baby with my abusive, alcoholic ex-husband, and was trapped in an abusive relationship with no one to turn to for help. I was watching the Ritz video where Axl gave the talk about not letting people tell you what to do and try to hold you back before "Out Ta Get Me" and the speech before "My Michelle" about holding onto your dream and believing. It literally was the swift kick in my ass that gave me the courage to escape my marriage and save the lives of my son and myself. My ex tried to kill me twice. I am eternally grateful to Axl for that and hope one day to be able to thank him in person.

I have been a fan for 30 years now and will remain a fan until I die. I can relate to so many of the songs on all of the albums. Looking back on that experience, I can say I definitely relate to "Better" too.

Motley Crue Fan: Tarja Koistila

Born and raised in Sweden, started listening to Motley Crue in my teens. Saw them every time they came to Sweden. Biggest dream was to see them on their home stage in LA. So at age 20 I left home and headed to LA. Signed up to be a live-in nanny, hated kids! Met Vince in 1988, dream came true!!

Bon Jovi Fan: Laurin, who runs social media fan pages for Matt Bon Jovi

When I was a teenager, my dad was transferred with his company and we had to move from Long Island to Orlando. My bff and I are HUGE Bon Jovi fans and I remember us crying soo hard and hugging soo tight and we kept saying "Holding on we gotta try, holding on to NEVER SAY GOODBYE" that was (and still, to this day) is our motto!!

She has always loved Jon but I've always been partial to Matt ever since I saw him as a kid when he was 13! I tried to start a fan club for him way back then! I wrote to him soo many times through the Bon Jovi fan club (secret society, which his mom ran). Finally, Matt called me! He got a kick out of the idea of a fan club for him and told me to go for it!

Well, I TRIED! I was 15 and had no idea how to go about starting one for him! I called all NY radio stations (obviously this was before I moved) but I couldn't get any to help me because Matty wasn't the "Famous" one! So my fan club never went anywhere.

Well, all these years later enter Twitter and Instagram! I finally was able to give Matt his fan page. And, lol, he doesn't even FOLLOW them!! I gotta wonder... does he even REMEMBER all those years ago?? I've sent messages but he doesn't answer me. Hmm.

Guns N' Roses Fan: Jonny Ferrari

Music is a huge part of my life, as with many people. However this genre defines me, my life, all the most personal details. Only Rock and Roll can do that. In the poker "hey days" we were the rock stars of Vegas.

Pink Floyd, as a celebrity entertainer and gaming figure certainly hits home with me. Many of times being alone in my Las Vegas penthouse using "unmentionables" ignoring girls, wallowing in my self-destructiveness. I was in fact comfortably numb. My girlfriends thinking I am cheating on the road, me calling to find "nobody home". How could she (in Pink Floyd the wall movie) and in my personal life, what up with women and great men on the road. Ask kid Rock because only God knows why.

Guns n' Roses to me is the only challenger to Pink Floyd as the greatest band to ever exist. Not only in their music but their "creative differences" causing them to disband and not play together since 1993 was sad. In Las Vegas 2011, "Guns n' Roses" at Hard Rock café. What a joke! Axel with some no name guys in animal masks, I left went home and broke stuff.

Luckily during the opening of my poker room in Asia, GNR (the REAL GNR) Axl, Duff and... SLASH reunited for the "Not in the Lifetime tour", oh man and I was front row center in Bangkok Thailand. There was nothing like it, these artists and their songs changed my life, defined it, affects my mood and reignites my memories. The greatest solos of all time David Gilmore "comfortably numb" and Slash "November Rain", they are not a head banger group (GNR) they are deep, empathetic with Axle having the greatest voice in history.

Ironically, guitarist for the metal group Snake Bite has my name. The only other notable Jonny Ferrari on Earth I know of. That rocks! Pun intended.

Bon Jovi Fan: German Mejia T (Twitter)
Well, I was young when I heard Living on a prayer on the radio for first time, by these days I left the army and I arrived home, that song gave me hope, happiness and I felt the sun shining on my face.

Bon Jovi Fan: Rosie (Twitter)
I was mesmerized the first time I saw the "Runaway" video. I was hooked since then! I also went to HS in Queens, NY and one of my classrooms overlooked the tiny radio station WAPP which is who played them first and gave them their break. I feel so connected to them because of that.

Bon Jovi Fan: Karen Holden (Twitter)
Going through a really rough spot when I heard Someday I'll Be Saturday Night. I was immediately encouraged by that song. After that. I listen to **@BonJovi** every night straight for three months.

Bon Jovi Fan: Lauren (Twitter)
I was seven. I remember it so clearly. My sister was 11 and brought the cassette tape home. We listened to it in her room forever and loved every moment. That is when I became a huge Bon Jovi lover for life. I will never forget that moment in time. Changed my life.

Bon Jovi Fan: Steve Alan Rotert (Twitter)
Thoughout my life I've learned what it means to *live on a prayer* and *what it takes* to get though some really tough times. Ultimately it helped me to

discover how bad things can get and see what means to rely on the one you love being open to change!

Def Leppard Fan: Daisy Bell
When I was 14 I was convinced I was the reincarnation of Steve Clark from Def Leppard. I had been convinced for a very long time that I was the reincarnation of SOMEONE from that era because I felt like I knew all the people. And even knew how I died. I knew "I" had been with a friend, fell asleep on a couch and the friend had left and that was it (this is exactly how he died according to the report). I also used to say it may have been drugs or booze but really "I died of a broken heart."

I felt this before I discovered DL and when I first read about him I cried. It didn't feel good. It wasn't like when people proudly claim to be the reincarnation of Cleopatra or Elvis. It felt like a leaden weight. I also didn't idolize him or have a crush on him.

There were no mixed or confused feelings. Although I did love Def Lep and their music. I stopped believing in reincarnation as I once did ages ago, but it feels like a part of him is always still with me. I think I still carry his pain somehow because I identified with him at such a young and vulnerable age. I find it hard now to watch footage of him and don't listen to DL like I used to as a teen, especially because strange coincidences still occur.

Recently I saw an interview with his old long-term fiancé, Lorelei Shellist, and she said, "really, he died of a broken heart," and I felt that same leaden weight I had when I was 14 for the rest of that evening.

Alberta Chris Sanders with Slaughter

Emily Scicchitano with Brian Forsythe (Kix)

Jennifer Butler with Jani Lane

Diego Muniz with Skid Row tattoo

John Solenberger – Kix tattoo

Pam Holly Bare – Motley Crue tattoo

Andy Wade – GnR fan!

Leroy Cass – Mark Slaughter

Karen Eveland – Nikki Sixx tattoo

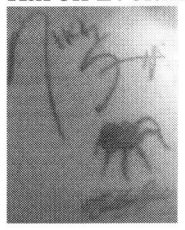

John Solenberger - Kix

Kevin Langlois – Lita Ford

Louie Vrzovski – Gene Simmons

Michael Shea – Buckcherry

Jan De Greve – Josh Todd, Buckcherry

Teresa Haller Hannah – Bobby Blotzer

Tanya Larry Reeder – Motley Crue tattoo

Jackie Davidson – Poison tattoo

Joan Chapman – Kix and Lynch Mob

Tara Janae – Blas Elias

Tony Gavigan – Ronnie Younkins (Kix)

Jennifer Elizabeth – Phil Lewis (L.A. Guns)

Jeannie Sweitzer – Scott Rockenfield (Queensryche)

Joan Chapman – Robby Lochner (Jack Russell)

David McCormick – Drew Hannah (Wildside)

Jeannie Sweitzer – Robert Mason

Sheila Kraemer – Tracii Guns (L.A. Guns)

Jan De Greve – Liv Sin (Sinster Sin)

Annemarie Buis – Dregen (Backyard Babies)

Joan Chapman – Marq Torien (BulletBoys)

Graham Blease – Mike Tramp (White Lion)

Joan Chapman – Michael Sweet (Stryper)

Sheila Kraemer – Rudy Sarzo (Whitesnake, Quiet Riot)

Jeannie Sweitzer – Janet Gardner (Vixen)

Joan Chapman - Kix

Teresa Haller Hannah – Joey Beladonna (Anthrax)

Jo Anne Bratkovich – Tracii Guns (L.A. Guns)

Tanya Larry Reeder – Taime Downe (Faster Pussycat)

Joan Chapman – Michael Grant

Stephanie Zermeno – Erik Turner (Warrant)

Judy Priston – Doug Aldrich (Whitesnake)

Jennifer Elizabeth – Taime Downe (Faster Pussycat)

Jane Ushwell Celebrity Gallery!

Kickin Valentina

Vinnie Paul

Vic Vino – Hardcore Superstar

Lexxi Foxx – Steel Panther

Simon Cruz

Olli Herman – Reckless Love

Phil Lewis – L.A. Guns

Jocke Berg – Hardcore Superstar

John Corabi

Steve Summers – Pretty Boy Floyd

Vain

George Lynch

Lemmy - Motorhead

ONLINE MUSIC SITES

Listed below are some of the best sites that cover the music we all love.

http://sleazeroxx.com/

http://www.blabbermouth.net

http://www.theglamnationnetwork.com/

http://www.theglamnationnetwork.com/

http://metalsludge.tv/

FACEBOOK PAGES

www.facebook.com/hairmetalmusic

https://www.facebook.com/80s-Hair-Band-and-Rock-and-Metal-Haven-252207694818853/?ref=br_rs

https://www.facebook.com/TOPGUNZ4488/

https://www.facebook.com/Hair-and-There-80s-Metal-80s-Hard-Rock-and-Classic-Rock-534099113365271/

https://www.facebook.com/hairmetalyears/

https://www.facebook.com/hmmofficial/

https://www.facebook.com/eightiesglamrock/

https://www.facebook.com/80sHairGlamMetalMusicForWorldAndLovers/

https://www.facebook.com/LongLive80sHairMetalGlammm/

https://www.facebook.com/80shairmetallovers/

https://www.facebook.com/hairmetalrnr/
https://www.facebook.com/80hairmetalbandnation/

https://www.facebook.com/80s-and-90s-hair-band-page-161213513973479/

https://www.facebook.com/HairBands4Ever/

https://www.facebook.com/80sHairGlamNation/?ref=br_rs

Printed in Great Britain
by Amazon